FIVE PORTRAITS

Rethinking Theory

FIVE PORTRAITS

*Modernity and
the Imagination
in Twentieth-Century
German Writing*

Michael André Bernstein

Northwestern University Press
Evanston, Illinois

Northwestern University Press
Evanston, Illinois 60208-4210

Printed in the United States of America

ISBN 0-8101-1774-6

Library of Congress Cataloging-in-Publication Data

Bernstein, Michael André, 1947—
    Five portraits: modernity and the imagination in twentieth-century German writing / Michael André Bernstein.
       p. cm.
       1. German literature—20th century—History and criticism. 2. Rilke, Rainer Maria, 1875–1926—Criticism and interpretation. 3. Musil, Robert, 1880–1942—Criticism and interpretation. 4. Heidegger, Martin, 1889–1976—Criticism and interpretation. 5. Benjamin, Walter, 1892–1940—Criticism and interpretation. 6. Celan, Paul—Criticism and interpretation. I. Title.

PT401.B47   2000
830.9'0091—dc21   00-008143

For Leo Löwenthal (1900–1993)
and
Amos Funkenstein (1937–1995)

Contents

Acknowledgments

Among the genuine pleasures of finishing a book, there are few as gratifying as the chance to express my appreciation for all the intelligence, time, and generous support from which I have benefited during its composition. The five portraits that make up this book were initially commissioned by Leon Wieseltier for the *New Republic*, and his careful editing and exacting scrutiny of each chapter were invaluable. I think that he sensed the existence of a coherent book in these initially discrete studies before I did, and his suggestions about which figures to write about next appear, retroactively at least, to have been made as much from the perspective of their potential place in such a book as from the exigencies of a specific occasion for his journal. I am very grateful both for his original instigation and for the right to reproduce the essays here.

Part of the introduction originally appeared in an essay published in *Modernism/Modernity*, whose editor, Robert von Hallberg, has long been a welcoming advocate of my work, and I am delighted to thank him both for permission to use my piece in this book and for the larger support that he has consistently offered me.

As I was working on these pieces, my close friend and colleague Robert Alter not only read and carefully commented on each one, but was always ready to throw himself into discussing whatever ideas and questions had me in their grip, no matter how far these were from his own immediate concerns and even when they risked distracting us from our weekly tennis game. His steadying advice, literary and stylistic acumen, and unwearying enthusiasm are a major example of the indispensable enterprise of integrating a love of literature with a richly shared communal life.

Since its first appearance in the *New Republic*, each of the chapters has been extensively revised and expanded, and during that process, I was extraordinarily fortunate to be able to draw on the advice, editorial skill, and seemingly limitless patience of a special circle of friends, colleagues, and students. M. E. Brugger, Gary Saul Morson, Dalya Michal Sachs, John A. DeWitt, Alex Zwerdling, Thomas G. Rosenmeyer, Brian Glaser, Margarita Yanson, and Elisabeth Demetz all helped make this book better than it could ever have been without their counsel. Susan Harris of Northwestern University Press was enthusiastic and helpful from the outset, and she has my genuine appreciation for her personal commitment to the project. Indeed, everyone else at the Press who contributed to the production of this book, especially Susan Betz and Maria Vettese, has been exemplary, and they amply deserve my thanks for their fine work.

Throughout my work on this book, there was nothing I missed as much as the chance to talk about its ideas with Leo Löwenthal and Amos Funkenstein. Often I would imagine to myself how they might react to my way of thinking about a problem or a specific formulation, and my dedicating the book to them is a small measure of how much their friendship meant to me and how much I continue to miss our conversations.

Introduction

Five Portraits and the Modernist Masterpiece

W hen Claude Lantier, a painter and the main character in Émile Zola's 1886 novel *L'Oeuvre*, cries out on returning to a canvas on which he has been working in vain, "It can kill me, it can kill my wife, it can kill my child, and it can kill the lot of us, but it will be a masterpiece, by God,"[1] perhaps the most disheartening thing about his words is their combination of febrile self-dramatization and utter conventionality. Far from expressing an unprecedented personal ambition—or even a unique pathology—by the time Lantier made his vow, it had already become a familiar slogan, one of the indispensable professions of faith necessary to confirm one's membership in the family of modernist geniuses.[2] Twenty years earlier, Flaubert's letters describing his hermitlike solitude at Croisset and the agonizing labor that went into every sentence of his novels had fixed the image of the modern writer as a deliberate martyr to his art and relegated whatever was not the product of a similar all-consuming dedication to the ranks of the second rate. But even if it is just to oneself that such affirmations must be made, and even if, like Lantier, one ends up honoring all of the covenant's grim terms, by the century's end, the sentiments and gestures are thoroughly formulaic and prescripted. The pledge does not so much accompany the production of a great work as it precedes and enables it, as though it were impossible even to begin the attempt at a modernist masterpiece without having undertaken such a commitment.

The impulse itself lasted long enough to be still clearly audible in Yeats's poem "The Choice," published in 1932: "The intellect of man is forced to choose / perfection of the life, or of the work."[3] A skeptical reader might wonder whether "perfection of the life" were really something that a human being could choose, or indeed what it might actually entail, but there is no doubt that Yeats, like Lantier almost half a century earlier, was convinced of an irreconcilable opposition between an artist's adventitious, personal existence and his hope of permanent achievements. Only the work matters, and the conflict between ordinary life and the all-consuming demands of art is framed by writers like Rilke and Yeats with an absolutism that would have seemed absurd before the nineteenth century. Undeniably, earlier artists had been equally concerned, programmatically and self-consciously, with the creation of enduring works. From Horace's certainty that his lines would outlast the ruler and city they ostensibly celebrate, to the innumerable Renaissance variations on the topos of the poet's bestowing immortality on an all too transitory lover, it is hardly necessary to recite a list of texts that carry clear evidence of their makers' hopes for a measure of permanent cultural centrality. But there *is* something essentially new about the terms in which modernist writers conceived of the project of masterpiece making, and the sense of the work's para-doxically destructive and redemptive relationship to quotidian human existence is among the principal differences.

Perhaps the most succinct way to trace the initial premises whose end result is the distinctive new form that I have called "the modernist masterpiece" is to go back to two nineteenth-century writers whose programmatic declarations would seem at first glance to share little with one another. In February 1844, Balzac wrote his lover and future wife, Éveline Hanska, a characteristically emphatic combination love letter and self-description: "This, in sum, is the game I am playing. Four men will have had an enormous life: Napoleon, Cuvier, O'Connell, and I intend to be the fourth. The first one lived the life of Europe; he engrafted himself to it through his armies! The second wedded the whole globe! The third made himself the incarnation of a people! And I—I shall have carried an entire society in my head!"[4] It is worth lingering for a moment on the carefully chosen range of Balzac's self-comparisons: (1) Napoléon Bonaparte, the parvenu whose conquests showed the virtually limitless potential of genius to, in effect, make a single individual's will the active principle of European history;[5] (2) Baron Cuvier (1769–1832), the celebrated naturalist whose work in comparative anatomy and systems of zoological classification led to novel ways of ordering, and thus understanding, life itself; (3) Daniel O'Connell (1775–1847), "the great Liberator" and champion of Catholic emancipation in Ireland, whose efforts on behalf of the disenfranchised made him "the incarnation of an entire people"; and, finally, (4) Balzac himself, the prodigious novelist whose ambition encompassed nothing less than the creation of a parallel, self-contained social and political totality, an imaginative project whose challenge was, at its most grandiose, *to compete with* (*faire concurrence à* is his expression) civil society.[6] The terms of Balzac's comparisons are no more accidental than is the all-embracing epic title *The Human Comedy*, which he finally chose for his sequence of novels, and by placing himself last in the list, he was also indicating both that his own work would unite, in a fundamentally new way, the distinctive energies of all three preceding figures, and that *The Human Comedy*, like Dante's *Divine* one, would eventually be seen as the summa of the century's most decisive accomplishments and aims.

Against this colossally ambitious self-definition, I would like to balance Stéphane Mallarmé's equally provocative announcements in "Crise De Vers": "Languages are imperfect precisely because there are several of them; the one supreme language is lacking . . . the very diversity of idioms on earth prevents one from uttering the words which otherwise would be, by a single articulation, the fullness of truth itself. This prohibition exists expressly . . . to eliminate any grounds for fantasizing oneself God."[7] It is a critical commonplace that no two writers could be further apart in method, craftsmanship, or intended audience than Balzac and Mallarmé. Yet what stands out in their programmatic declarations is the unprecedented insistence with which they both claimed for their art the power to create a separate world, in every sense as comprehensive as the realm of quotidian reality. Or, as Mallarmé put it with characteristic absolutism in "Le Livre, Instrument Spirituel," "everything in the world exists to culminate in *one* book" (*tout, au monde, existe pour aboutir à un livre*).[8] Not in "*a* book," as the words are invariably translated, but rather in *one* unique and all-encompassing text that will absorb not just all prosaic objects and events, but also every single prior artistic creation. Mallarmé's quasi-mystical meditation on "the one supreme language" in which "the fullness of truth itself" would find expression directly inspired some of Walter Benjamin's most searching comments on the nature of language, and it has haunted every modernist writer possessed by what Benjamin called the dream of "integrating many tongues into one true language."[9] For such longings, the sheer multiplicity of poems and languages is an implicit rebuke. In principle, there can only be *one* ultimate text, "Le Livre," and hence only *one* language in which the entire anarchic raw material of separate human discourses would be incorporated, transformed, and made whole again. If the decline into separate texts is a permanent reminder of how far we are from divinity, it also issues what amounts to a cosmic challenge to undo the Fall by inventing a new tongue in which the lost totality of separate discourses could be synthesized anew, and it contains the startling implication that such inventiveness would be quite literally a God-like act.

It is the enormity of the stakes claimed for the modernist masterpieces that underlies the self-destructive wager of an aspirant like Lantier. But these same premises also propel many of the most successful modernist works and provide the horizon of expectations for each successive attempt. The project confronting the makers of a modernist masterpiece was not really commensurate with the efforts of even their most ambitious predecessors, in part because the category of the whole had become essentially arbitrary: one could accept, in other words, the abstract goal of what Wagner had called a "total work of art" (*Gesamtkunstwerk*), but since there was no more cultural agreement on what constituted a coherent totality in the first place, each artist was compelled to determine his own particular, and thus necessarily idiosyncratic, selection. But after Balzac, Wagner, and Mallarmé, the entire logic of the all-embracing masterpiece makes any acknowledgment of its arbitrariness inadmissible, so the new work must not only select its *materia poetica* from a range of possibilities and with an absence of generic guidelines hitherto unthinkable, it must do so in such a way as to make that selection appear simultaneously inevitable and complete. One way to make the stakes—and the strains—of such a project more explicit is to isolate three imperatives that both define and propel the modernist masterpiece. My argument, to express the matter as concisely and unqualifiedly as possible, is that it was absolutely essential for the work to *claim* to fulfill these imperatives—that they are, in fact, the necessary categories of the modernist masterpiece as such—but that for powerful logical and historical reasons they remained, in actuality, impossible to satisfy. What emerged out of the tension between the fulfillment and the frustration of these demands is precisely what we have come to recognize as the characteristic triumphs and particular problems of the modernist masterpiece as a distinct and historically circumscribed form.

1. It Must Seem Universal

As a heterogeneous new form, the modernist masterpiece cuts across conventional genre divisions, and its lineaments can be traced as readily in philosophical texts like Wittgenstein's *Tractatus Logico-Philosophicus* and Heidegger's *Being and Time* as in paintings, works of literature, or musical compositions. In each instance, though, what is indispensable is that by its resonance, implication, and significance, the modernist masterpiece makes clear that no matter how gritty its narrative may be with the texture of local details, and no matter how autobiographically determined the selection of its specific settings and themes, its true reach is global and all-encompassing. Thus, for example, Joyce has to insist that "Ulysses/Bloom is the *only* complete all-round character presented by any writer."[10] In this regard, too, one can see Sigmund Freud's project as the creation of a special sort of modernist masterpiece. Freud's theorizing increasingly laid claim to an all-inclusive understanding of human nature and civilization, not just of the individual psyches of his patients. Freud's *Standard Edition* is thus not only his encyclopedic masterpiece, it is a remarkably Balzacian one. Throughout the Freudian corpus, a few specific figures (the "Case Histories") function as both exemplary instances and pedagogic models for a theory of humanity as a whole, so that Dora, the Wolf-Man, Little Hans, and the Rat-Man have a very similar function in Freud's *Standard Edition* to that occupied by Rastignac, Vautrin, César Birotteau, Louis Lambert, and the other central characters in *La Comédie humaine*.

No matter what the genre, though, everything in the modernist masterpiece must be presented so as to remove any sense that an individual author's temperament, interests, and background are responsible for the inclusion of just *these* details, for the selection of just *these* puns, ideograms, or mythic parallels. The belated critical catchphrase "death of the author"[11] is best understood not as a global pronouncement about writing or subjectivity as such, but as a specific technical device intended to safeguard the authority of the work from any trace of "mere individuality," an individuality which must always, in this context, carry the mark of an unacceptable arbitrariness. One way to enact at least a simulacrum of this precarious balancing act between the local and the universal is to establish a kind of imaginative apostolic succession in which the new work is seen as the rightful successor of the masterpieces that preceded it, and the early years of this century showed an unprecedented use of classical myth for just this purpose. The modernists' widespread reliance on mythological materials is ultimately less important for its specific thematic or even structuring function than as a means of asserting two indispensable, general claims: namely, that (1) the new masterpiece is the legitimate present-day incarnation of the culture's foundational texts and topoi, and (2) its alertness to the contingencies of the present is congruent with its status as already an incipient classic. Baudelaire, in a passage central to Benjamin as well, defined the secret ambition of modern art in exactly these terms: "it longs to be worthy of itself becoming antiquity."[12] Linked to this strategy, but logically independent of it, is the decision to make palpable the text's universality by creating a new kind of language for it, one that will embody, in its very articulation, the universalist claims of the narrative. Ultimately, not just the work's characters and events but even its language will be drawn, in the wonderful formula of *Finnegans Wake*, from "all marryvoising moodmoulded cyclewheeling history."[13]

2. It Must Be Difficult

"I've put in so many enigmas and puzzles that it will keep the professors busy for centuries arguing over what I meant, and that's the only way of insuring one's immortality."[14] Literary critics are continuing to pile up hecatombs of explanatory volumes that demonstrate the justice of Joyce's words. But his comment must once have rung far odder than we can easily recognize today. The changing role of the university and the very success of the modernist masterpiece as a project have tended to "naturalize" Joyce's longing to be argued over by academics and obscured just how far-fetched Joyce's hope was when he first uttered it in 1921. At that time, contemporary literature was not part of any university curriculum and not likely to become such, either. When modernist artists put in their "enigmas and puzzles," they were not so much anticipating, but to a significant degree actively *creating* the situation Joyce's phrase seems only to describe. The modernist masterpieces were composed from the outset with the intention of being *studied*, not just read, and their way of advancing such seemingly preposterous expectations required what one might call "a strategy of presumptive immortality."[15] Modernist masterpiece making entails creating an entirely new scholarly and critical context in which the works will be received, and this requirement is a constituent part of the whole project, directly affecting the composition of the piece itself.

In a paradoxical return of the repressed, the values of bourgeois probity and industriousness against which artists had proclaimed themselves in rebellion throughout the nineteenth century were transferred largely intact to the aesthetic sphere. Instead of the *sprezzatura* valued by earlier periods, modernist masterpieces were expected to exhibit the scars of their enormous difficulty. I am inclined to think that the only realm in which Marx's labor theory of value is at all convincing is in the domain of the modernist masterpiece, where the labor of the artist earns the right to exact a reciprocal effort on the part of the reader. Ultimately, the reader's willingness to undertake that labor depends on his already having accepted the principle that a masterpiece is entitled to make such extraordinary demands. Whether any particular work merits the designation of a masterpiece is open to debate, but never the independent existence of the category itself. Joyce's typically modernist motif of the artist-as-God works precisely because in the unprecedented breadth, depth, and extent of his representation of their existence, he can make his characters totally legible and, correspondingly, leave his readers totally subservient to the fullness of his knowledge. In this sense, writing the modernist literary or philosophical masterpiece is eerily akin to what James C. Scott has recently called the "high modernist" imposition of mammoth economic and social engineering projects in agriculture, city planning, and compulsory rural resettlement by "visionary" leaders certain of their insight into what the population required.[16] Although Scott himself does not invoke literary analogies, his argument that since the start of the nineteenth century, governments have increasingly tried to make the life of society fully "legible" in order to make it comprehensible, and hence manageable, fits Balzac's novelistic intentions in *La Comédie humaine* as readily as it does the political ones of such countries' rulers. In the same vein, the map of Yoknapatawpha County at the back of *Absalom, Absalom!* is clearly marked "William Faulkner, Sole Owner and Proprietor," and the witty variant on customary declarations of authorial copyright and lack of legal liability to outside parties scarcely tempers the seriousness of Faulkner's claim. What makes the whole project particularly strange in the case of theoretical and literary texts, however, is that although the necessary fiction of works like *Being and Time, The Origin of German Tragic Drama,* or *Finnegans Wake* is that we are being taught how to read a new kind of universal idiom, what we are actually acquiring instead is a discrete and nontransferable fluency in a series of heterogeneous, radically incommensurable works. Indeed, learning how to make sense of any one modernist masterpiece is of remarkably little help in being able to understand a different one. Each new modernist masterpiece returns one to the position of a neophyte struggling to comprehend mysteries whose significance must be taken on faith since they can be grasped only after a sufficient expenditure of labor, much of which will at first be conducted in ignorance of what one is learning. But that very effort to acquire even a preliminary interpretative competence with any particular work encourages a self-protective, mutually confirming loyalty to a project in which both artist and audience have already invested so much. The Absolute Artist now requires something like an Abject Reader whose devotion to the modernist masterpiece is both self-abnegating and all consuming. Or, as Joyce said, not all that playfully, to Max Eastman, "The demand that I make of my reader is that he should devote his whole life to reading my works."[17]

3. It Must Be Redemptive

What ultimately justifies Flaubert's self-immurement in Croisset, and what, presumably, would have justified Lantier had he been able to produce his masterpiece, is the paradoxical fact that such a sacrifice would ultimately have enriched life itself and made even the moments of total misery retroactively meaningful. Leo Bersani has coined the helpful phrase "the culture of redemption" to describe the idea that art exists to give value to, and thus to salvage, an otherwise meaningless existence. Only art, in the form of a timeless masterpiece, can restore and make whole all the suffering, triviality, and wastefulness of life.[18] From Mallarmé's longing to absorb the world into a single Book to Rilke's joyful inward re-creation of a fractured and alienated existence, the bedrock certainty about the redemptive power of great art remains constant. Although the disruptions, incompleteness, and fragmentation of so many modernist masterpieces function, at the heart of the texts themselves, as a kind of immanent critique of the project, they do not ironize it through the stance and topos of humor, but rather through the darker ones of failure and the fear of failure. The modernist masterpiece, that is, can ironize everything except its own desire to be one. Masterpieces may be pluralistic texts, but *faith* in masterpieces is the strictest of monotheisms.

Each of my three imperatives presents the modernist masterpiece with a challenge that it is certain not to meet entirely, both because the demands are inherently unattainable and because if any work had succeeded, it would have constituted the unique, all-embracing achievement for which everyone was striving, thereby obviating the need for further attempts. But the utter discrediting of the last of my three categories, even as a theoretically desirable goal, allows us to date the end of the project as a whole with a specificity altogether unusual for imaginative undertakings. From the moment the horrors of history came to be regarded as so cataclysmic that any idea of their being somehow "redeemed" through art seemed obscene, the whole foundation of the modernist masterpiece was no longer credible. Our knowledge of the Nazi genocide and the decades-long horror of the Gulag has fundamentally eroded the myth of art's all-absorptive, all-transfiguring power. The death factories, killing fields, and slave labor camps of the Third Reich and Soviet Russia have become like boundary lines marking the limits of art's redemptive claims. Ambitious and enduring imaginative works have continued to be produced in every genre after the liberation of the concentration camps in 1945, just as they were before the modernist masterpiece emerged as a new form. But they are not modernist masterpieces in the sense I have tried to define here. The modernist masterpiece as a coherent project extends only from Mallarmé to Paul Celan, and it is the very fact that its epoch has now passed that allows us to delineate clearly its defining features and historical trajectory.

The initial thrust of that much-contested and increasingly threadbare catch-word "postmodernism" arises from the systematic subversion of all three of the imperatives I have just listed. Such a critique dismisses the idea that art can redeem lost time or damaged lives, and it counters assertions of the masterpiece's universality with an insistence that every work explicitly acknowledge its own historicity and "partiality." At its most radical, it throws into doubt the category of the genius, which from Kant to Duchamp, and especially in Rilke, Joyce, Proust, and Heidegger, grounded and justified the particular exempla the writer chose, exempla whose universality was guaranteed precisely and tautologically because they were discovered by a genius. Stephen Dedalus's proud claim "A man of genius makes no mistakes. His errors are volitional and are the portals of discovery" is uncomfortably consonant with Heidegger's self-glorifying defense of all his lapses, presumably also including his early support for Nazism: "He who thinks greatly must err greatly" (*Wer denkt gross, muss gross irren*).[19] The ideology of the genius upon which these assertions and the very possibility of a modernist masterpiece both depend could not survive what happened to humankind in and through the German language between 1933 and 1945.

It should be obvious that I am far from suggesting a necessary connection between modernist writers and any of the century's sinister political movements. But I am deeply interested in how the figure of the inspired genius and the corollary question of the cult of inwardness function in the modern imagination. That they do so at the level of both high and popular culture, as well as that of politics, seems indisputable. With characteristic astuteness, Musil recognized that "Long before the dictators, our times brought forth spiritual veneration of dictators. Stefan George, for instance. Then Kraus and Freud, Adler and Jung as well. Add to these Klages and Heidegger."[20] The readiness to sacrifice not just one's own, but, equally, everyone else's welfare in order to realize a personal vision is *the* archetypal impulse of the modernist genius, and it is equally traceable in aesthetic doctrines, intellectual debates, and political programs. It is just this readiness that links Zola's Lantier and Joyce's Stephen Dedalus to the radical modernizers in other spheres, including the Soviet leader Lenin, the architect Le Corbusier, and the African statesman Julius Nyerere, all three of whose ideas and policies are analyzed as quintessential instances of high modernism in Scott's *Seeing Like a State*. Whether in the realm of politics, art, or philosophy, part of a genius's charisma is his ability to offer acolytes the privilege of participating in the spell of his matchless inspiration. What Hitler called the *Führerprinzip*, the right of the superior being to the unquestioning obedience of others, is dependent on a culturally shared mythologization of the genius's unique insight, and its charismatic power is inextricably bound up with the history of modernism itself.

The thrill of feeling oneself caught up in such a vision—even, or perhaps *especially*, at the cost of one's own self-interest—can be as indispensable an aspect of aesthetic or intellectual discipleship as of political adherence. The success of any *Führerprinzip* requires the mobilization in others of a matching *Folgerprinzip*, or delight in total obedience. But the fact that versions of the same tropes, elicited by and directed toward very different kinds of people, can trigger powerful identificatory fantasies as readily in the cultured salons and university seminars as in the crowds at a mass rally, does not make them in any way ethically equivalent, let alone comparable in their historical consequences. It does, however, suggest the need to probe the history and inner workings of that identificatory self-surrender and its relationship to the notion of inwardness with more care than the subject has customarily received.

Although the modernist masterpiece was a thoroughly international phenomenon without a geographic center or native language, nowhere was the question of the relationship among its artistic, intellectual, and political aspects more fraught than in the German-speaking world. The idioms of visionary inwardness and of apocalyptic destruction were both realized in German with unparalleled single-mindedness, as were, just to complicate the picture, some of the most lucid critiques of both impulses. The five portraits that follow are an attempt, partial and fragmentary, as befits their limited compass, to explore these relationships in the works of a particular constellation of diverse writers and thinkers. The group includes two poets, a novelist, a philosopher, and a literary and cultural theoretician, and their careers span the entire length of the modernist masterpiece's initial elaboration, its full flourishing, and its ultimate collapse. Equally important, because the issues raised were never confined within strictly national boundaries, the figures represented are, as my title makes clear, German-language writers, not German-national ones. Indeed, of the five, only Heidegger and Benjamin were German citizens. Rilke and Musil were born and spent much of their lives as Habsburg subjects in the multinational Austro-Hungarian Empire, while Paul Celan was born in the immediate aftermath of that empire's disintegration in Bukovina, a province that had passed from Austria-Hungary to Romania only two years before his birth.

In his reflections "On the Essay," Musil says that the arguments and connections set into play in an essay "are in many cases only a singularity. There is no total solution, but only a series of particular ones."[21] My own critical practice in this book is based on a similar conviction, and I have no wish to claim that the particular studies offered here coalesce into anything like the "group portrait" of a whole era or that they isolate a unified and stable set of themes. But focusing on a series of major German-language writers as simultaneously self-reflective and ambitious as these five does offer the potential for a series of linked speculations on the complex interplay between the apocalyptic and the prosaic strains in modernism. No doubt a different combination of authors would have required a different critical palette and highlighted other lines of affiliations and shared motifs. But that recognition does not undermine the aim of these essays so much as it invites other voices to enter into a dialogue with them and make a more complete gallery by adding to it the results of their own differing interests, methodologies, and chosen subjects.

For many years, there was a sign in the Vienna Opera House, MITSINGEN NICHT ERLAUBT, which warned the audience not to attempt to sing along with the performers. It is a caution that would not be out of place on critical texts as well, especially for studies dealing with Heidegger, Benjamin, and Celan. Too much of the commentary about these writers is still couched in a kind of lumpen version of their discourse, as though involuntary rhetorical mimesis were an index of comprehension and intelligent sympathy. I have tried to avoid falling into such habits and hope that this book will be accessible to readers who are not specialists in one or another of the figures it treats. Certainly the whole genre of the literary-intellectual portrait, a genre practiced brilliantly by several of the authors analyzed here, has become distinctly unfashionable, and I admit to a certain polemical intent in trying to contribute to its revival. But contrary to much of what is considered "advanced" thinking in contemporary criticism, I believe that the role of theory should be only to illuminate practice, never to dictate it, and the provisional, essayistic mode of the portrait as a form is especially congenial to such an aim. My guiding hope is that through the juxtaposition of the separate portraits with and against one another in a single volume, a new kind of conversation becomes audible in which the contradictory voices of five preternaturally strong writers can be heard with a clarity and uncoerciveness that would be far harder to bring out if each were treated in isolation. At the very least, tracing the conflicting passions and perspectives of these writers in one volume brings one up sharply before a simple sentence of Musil's that not only serves as an instigation for the essayistic thinking that is the indispensable corrective to every larger ambition, including that of this study, but also stands as a salutary reminder of the fragility of all our judgments: "I have always known that whatever one thinks will somehow sooner or later be wrong."[22]

1

Rainer Maria Rilke
The Book of Inwardness

An incessant self-mythologizing and an unmistakable authenticity collided in Rilke's writing virtually from the beginning. For years, hand-me-down poses and a derivative rhetoric contended with a strikingly new lyric voice and purpose, the two almost embarrassingly audible at every level of the verse. In 1899, for example, at the end of an early cycle of linked poems, *The Book of Monastic Life*, Rilke adopts the voice of a simple monk who has seen a figure of power—angel or divinity—enter his cell:

> Ich seh ihn sitzen und sinnen,
> nicht über mich hinaus;
> für ihn ist alles innen,
> Himmel und Heide und Haus.[1]

> I see him sitting and musing
> not beyond me;
> for him, everything is within—
> heaven and heath and house.

What is startling about these early lines is not their technical clumsiness, but rather how thoroughly they already express the grounding premise of his mature poetics. The conviction that the entire natural world in all its richness can be transformed and re-created in the inner consciousness of a higher being is one from which Rilke would never swerve; but at this stage, the gap between his technique and the poem's claims appears almost unbridgeable. Even if the heavy, full rhymes, straightforward rhythm, vague diction, and overinsistent repetitions of basic sound units like "i" and "n" can be justified as appropriate to the naive monk who is the poem's speaker, they are all thoroughly commonplace devices, and they recur throughout the early volumes, irrespective of the poem's specific occasion or theme.

For this reason, the standard accounts of Rilke's career place great emphasis upon the supposedly fundamental change in his writing after he moved to Paris in 1902 and began his self-imposed apprenticeship to Auguste Rodin. To his wife, Clara, Rilke wrote how profoundly he had been affected by Rodin's patient, workmanlike dedication to his art, his unmatched combination of delicacy, objectivity, and monumentality, and his mastery of making even fragmentary pieces of sculpture seem quick with life. Almost immediately, though, Rilke expands the most lapidary of Rodin's phrases into elaborate parables about how an artist should live, cautionary tales that quickly begin to sound more like Rilke's already long-held opinions than like anything his mentor would say:

> *"Il faut travailler, rien que travailler. Et il faut avoir patience."* [One must work, only work. And one must have patience.] You should not think of wanting to *do* anything, you should only try to build up your own means of expression so as to say everything. You should work and have patience. Look neither to the right nor left. Draw your whole life into this circle, have *nothing* outside this life. . . . You must sacrifice all else . . . : you must choose . . . either happiness or art. *On doit trouver le bonheur dans son art.* [One must find one's happiness in one's art.] . . . All the great men have let their lives get overgrown like an old path and have carried everything into their art. Their life is stunted like an organ they no longer use. . . . Rodin has lived nothing that is not his work. . . . This is the essential, that you should not stop at dreams, at intentions, at being in the mood, but that you should transpose everything into *things* with all your strength. As Rodin has done. . . . doing, doing, that's the thing. . . . When Rodin walks around among his things you feel how youth, certainty and new work are continually streaming into him from them. . . . His work stands like a great angel at his side and protects him.[2]

Rilke had arrived in Paris knowing that the subjective, impressionistic technique of his first books was too insubstantial to sustain a lifetime's work and that he needed to discipline himself to achieve some of the objective solidity of form and feeling that he found in Rodin's "art of living surfaces." The astounding outpouring of closely observed, syntactically complex, and passionately impersonal descriptions of animals, dancers, fountains, and statues that fill the two volumes of *New Poems* of 1907 and 1908 are a triumphant vindication of Rilke's determination and craftsmanship.

And yet, the crucial first volume of these so-called *Dinggedichte,* or "thing-poems," culminates in an image of a bowl of roses whose magical gift of trans-

forming the whole world around them and refashioning it into their own pure
interiority is uncannily reminiscent of the very assumptions Rilke is routinely said
to have left behind:

> Und sind nicht alle so, nur sich enthaltend,
> wenn Sich-enthalten heißt: die Welt da draußen
> und Wind und Regen und Geduld des Frühlings
> und Schuld und Unruh und vermummtes Schicksal
> und Dunkelheit der abendlichen Erde
> bis auf der Wolken Wandel, Flucht und Anflug,
> bis auf den vagen Einfluß ferner Sterne
> in eine Hand voll Innres zu verwandeln.
> "Die Rosenschale"

> And aren't all [the roses] that way, containing just themselves,
> if self-containing means: to change the world outside
> and wind and rain and patience of the spring
> and guilt and restlessness and muffled fate
> and the darkness of the evening earth
> out to the changing and flying and fleeing of the clouds
> and the vague influence of distant stars
> into a hand full of inwardness.
> "The Bowl of Roses"[3]

"To change the world into a hand full of inwardness." Great poets never entirely
abandon the impulses and perceptions that prompted their first compositions.
No matter how they may distance themselves from the language in which they
originally formulated them, and irrespective of the immensely greater technical
skill with which they learn to express themselves, the original intuitions are too
much a part of any poet's makeup to be simply left behind. A year later, Rilke admits
to Lou Andreas-Salomé that he took from Rodin only what he himself had already
set out to find.[4] Among the true mysteries of Rilke's genius is how many of his early
poems' most pedestrian characteristics go on, in a remarkably short time, to provide
the foundation for a whole series of major works. Lists of unadorned substantives,
nouns often linked by nothing but meter or alliteration, figure centrally in all his
writing, from the first book until the final poems, but they acquire an incremental,
gradually increasing emotional and conceptual density as their context validates
their significance and endows them with ever greater resonance. Although images
like "heaven, heath and house" seem emptily formulaic in *The Book of Monastic
Life*, these same words, when they reappear charged with meaning in so many
of the great poems of subsequent decades, do so in the identical role they had

failed to fulfill originally: for Rilke, these simple noun-strings will always be the unabandonable, talismanic icons of a fully internalized universe whose celebration constitutes what he means by poetry itself.

As late as the Ninth Duino Elegy, completed in 1922, Rilke will again declare:

Sind wir vielleicht *hier*, um zu sagen: Haus,
Brücke, Brunnen, Tor, Krug, Obstbaum, Fenster,—
höchstens: Säule, Turm . . .

Perhaps we are *here* in order to say house,
bridge, fountain, gate, pitcher, fruit-tree, window,—
at most: column, tower . . .[5]

Here, just knowing how to say these simple nouns with the requisite care has become a kind of synecdoche of the attentiveness with which the *Elegies* urge us to regard the entire created world. There is scarcely any difference in the specific content of the many lists in the *Duino Elegies* from the one spoken by the monk in *The Book of Monastic Life*; what has changed utterly, though, is the poet's recognition of the difficulty we have in giving such words any inward meaning at all in a world where, as the *Elegies* lament, we are so little at home. In a sense, Rilke's own laborious trajectory from the mechanical list making in *The Book of Monastic Life* to the Adamic naming of the *Duino Elegies* provides the implicit model that must be followed if we are to fulfill the task of "saying" the world. At the end of the quest, though, the transformation of world into word, or rather their interpenetration, resembles nothing so much as the spiritual condition of the angelic visitor already described by Rilke's monk two decades earlier. In this regard, perhaps the most self-referentially triumphant assertion in all the *Elegies* is the moment in the Seventh Elegy when the speaker declares:

Nirgends, Geliebte, wird Welt sein, als innen.

Nowhere, beloved, will world be but within.[6]

No doubt that inward re-creation of the world is potentially available at any moment and for anyone. Rilke even tells us that it can be accomplished more readily in the folds of a rose or the gaze of an animal than in the alienated consciousness of a human being, but we, Rilke's readers, are witnessing it take place in the very poem that has made itself simultaneously the herald of that task and its fulfillment. The *Elegies'* praise of inwardness takes up the root impulse of Rilke's earliest poetry, as well as of all the volumes in between, as though, like the T. S. Eliot of the

Four Quartets, Rilke, too, makes little distinction between endings and beginnings, certain that "the end of all our exploring / Will be to arrive where we started / And to know the place for the first time."[7]

None of Rilke's readers has been more sensitive to the profound continuity in his art than Robert Musil. In his 1927 "Address at the Memorial Service for Rilke in Berlin" (an address he delivered on behalf of the city's leading writers, over the vehement objections of Bertolt Brecht), Musil saw in Rilke's career a continuous enlargement of formal resources united to a singleness of vision discernible in each of the poet's different phases. Instead of the conventional view of a radical break separating the early from the later verse, Musil points to the subtle connections linking volumes from different periods and poetic idioms in Rilke's output. For Musil, who usually viewed his contemporaries with acerbic distaste, Rilke was simply "the greatest lyric poet the Germans have seen since the Middle Ages,"[8] and that judgment has been so widely accepted now that it is hard to remember it was once a matter of intense public controversy.

Rilke, along, perhaps, with William Butler Yeats, Robert Frost, and Hayyim Nahman Bialik, is among the very few major twentieth-century poets whose eminence in the eyes of other writers has been matched by a widespread and enduring popularity. At the time of Rilke's death on December 29, 1926, for example, his 1905 volume *The Book of Hours* had already sold nearly 59,000 copies. What is still more telling, neither his critical nor his popular appeal has diminished in the seventy years since then.[9] While the work of most of his contemporaries has been subject to recurring cycles of reappraisal, Rilke has become identified with the essential nature of poetry itself, his lines so deeply embedded in the common memory that they almost serve a similar collective function as the great anonymous compositions of oral cultures. Its very intimacy and air of radical solitude, its lack of overt solicitation to ordinary human dialogue, has made of Rilke's poetry a new kind of tale of the tribe, one that marshals its readers' deepest identification not by engaging public issues but by seeming to voice their own most inward concerns. No poet before Rilke had insisted as forcefully that solitude is itself a fundamental human need, and as the space of any genuine privacy began to narrow under the pressure of twentieth-century political and economic standardization, that insistence seemed not only prescient but deeply salutary.

The fact that this same inwardness and solitude is not without a strong component of self-pity is no doubt part of its abiding appeal. Who has not wanted to hear his or her own loneliness and melancholy given memorable form? There is no more perfect instantiation of Rilke's half-mournful, half-welcoming depiction of this mood than the end of the poem "Autumn Day" from 1902. Probably none of Rilke's stanzas has been quoted as often or identified with more directly:

Wer jetzt kein Haus hat, baut sich keines mehr.
Wer jetzt allein ist, wird es lange bleiben,
wird wachen, lesen, lange Briefe schreiben
und wird in den Alleen hin und her
unruhig wandern, wenn die Blätter treiben.

"Herbsttag"

Who has no house now, will never build one.
Who is alone now, will long remain so,
will stay awake, read, write long letters
and will wander restlessly up and down
the tree-lined streets, when the leaves are drifting.

"Autumn Day"[10]

In only three years separating "Autumn Day" from *The Book of Monastic Life*, Rilke's craftsmanship had increased immeasurably, but his new mastery is not signaled by any kind of wholesale discarding of an initial repertoire that poets like Ezra Pound and William Carlos Williams imposed on themselves. Instead, it is effected by the slightest of modulations: the rhymes stay as sonorous as before, but in place of the earlier, predictable *a-b-a-b* quatrains governing much of his first books, Rilke's shift to a final five-line stanza, after two earlier stanzas of first three and then four lines each, permits an imbalanced *a-b-b-a-b* sequence to orchestrate the poem's closure. Since our ears and eyes register the asymmetry in the rhyme scheme as well as in the stanza lengths, this blending of formal completion and unresolved disparities in the poem's structure is crucial in creating a mood that unites restlessness and resignation. It is worth emphasizing, as well, how directly the poem's subtle emotional effects depend upon relatively straightforward and immediately graspable technical decisions. Consider, for example, how the tightly balanced hemistiches of the first two lines are each dominated by a caesura that triggers, at the level of meter and syntax, the very rupture the words are expressing, and how this formal symmetry sets up the antithesis between poise and abandonment, between melodic control and emotional helplessness, that is the wellspring of the poem's haunting fluency.

With his fondness for full rhymes and relatively uncomplicated syntax, Rilke's early verse is often easily memorizable, and since much of the best-known modern poetry is not, we have tended to underestimate how potent a resource that can be. The sense of almost instantaneous and unmediated intimacy that readers frequently feel with Rilke owes a great deal to the speed with which they can hear his lines in their own minds without needing to look at any external printed text. (Revealingly enough, none of Rilke's syntactically complex, unrhymed poetry has achieved anything like the same degree of general popularity.) In this sense, the readers' response to the poetry exactly duplicates the transformation of everything outside oneself into part of one's own inner being that Rilke believed was the poet's chief task. But there is also something immensely flattering to the reader in having internalized a great poet's lines, since it turns the writer's words, as well as his sentiments and sensibility, into the reader's own.

Knowing a poem "by heart" can make it feel almost like a joint creation whose words have arisen out of one's innermost depths. It is as though the whole authority of the poem's language and music had been summoned up primarily out of one's own tormented antinomies, and encountering one of Rilke's texts can feel less like reading an independent work of art than like suddenly receiving the gift of a magically exteriorized and heightened autobiography. Since they give one so powerful a sense of being able to overhear one's own innermost musings, Rilke's writings have inspired a degree of devotion in which it is not always easy to distinguish reverence for the artist from the reader's self-love.

For the generations of German readers raised on the intensities of Romantic poets like Novalis and Hölderlin, the thrill of participating in a poet's sacerdotal mission was overwhelmingly seductive. If Rilke's "inwardness" was the infallible sign of his fitness for that role, a reader's "inward" responsiveness was correspondingly laudable. From the turn of the century until today, being able to recite poems like "Autumn Day," or "Archaic Torso of Apollo," with its luminous ending "Du mußt dein Leben ändern" (You must change your life),[11] has offered a kind of spiritual patent of nobility, certifying the sensitivity of one's soul. The word *Innigkeit*, or "inwardness," has always carried strong religious and aesthetic connotations in English and in German, and its uses have ranged from John Wycliffe's fourteenth-century translation of Luke 1:78 ("Bi the inwardness of the merci of oure God")[12] to Beethoven's markings in several of his late piano sonatas (as, for example, *Gesangvoll, mit innigster Empfindung* in opus 109).

In Rilke, however, the long history of this term acquires its most radical meaning: "inwardness" now comes to signify not just a personal mood or condition, but the fulfilling of the earth's deepest dreams by internalizing the totality of creation.

> Erde, ist es nicht dies, was du willst: *unsichtbar*
> in uns erstehn? . . .
> Was, wenn Verwandlung nicht, ist dein drängender Auftrag?
> > "Die neunte Elegie"

> Earth, isn't this what you want: to arise within us,
> *invisible?* . . .
> What, if not transformation, is your urgent command?
> > Ninth Elegy[13]

This transformation is also, as Rilke explains in letter after letter, his sole purpose in existing: "appearance and vision everywhere merged in the object, in each a whole interior world was revealed, as though an angel who encompassed all space were blind and gazing into himself. This, a world no longer seen from the standpoint of people, but *in* the angel, is perhaps my real task."[14] It is worth lingering on these words to emphasize how intransigently Rilke insists that his life only has significance once it has been entirely dedicated to a transcendent mission. By comparison, all the other difficult "tasks" of existence, including the responsibilities of a father, a lover, or a friend, are nothing but meaningless lures that distract the poet from his obligation to his art. Inwardness, which was originally cherished as the quintessential index of our common humanity, demands for Rilke nothing less than a leap beyond the human into an altogether different—and clearly superior—order of being.

Not surprisingly, the facility with which German culture has appropriated, and often misused, so pliant and highly charged a concept as "inwardness" has elicited strong counterreactions. The most relentlessly lucid of these critiques is Hannah Arendt's ferocious attack on the ethical bankruptcy of inwardness in her study of Rahel Varnhagen (1771–1833), the famous Berlin literary hostess who converted from Judaism to Protestantism after her marriage. For Arendt, the romantic cultivation of inwardness is deeply, indeed necessarily, linked both to self-deception and to a crippling misjudgment about the nature of the external world. As Arendt writes:

> [I]f thinking rebounds back upon itself and finds its solitary object within the soul—if, that is, it becomes introspection—it distinctly produces . . . a semblance of unlimited power . . . by the very act of isolation from the world . . . it also sets up a bastion in front of the one "interesting" object: the inner self [*das eigene Innere*] . . . In the isolation achieved by introspection thinking becomes limitless because it is no longer molested by anything exterior; because there is no longer any demand for action, the consequences of which necessarily impose limits even upon the freest spirit. Man's autonomy becomes hegemony over all possibilities . . . Reality can offer nothing new; introspection has already anticipated everything. Even the blows of fate can be escaped by flight into the self if every single misfortune has already been generalized beforehand as an inevitable concomitant of the bad outside world . . . Thus the power and the autonomy of the soul are secured. Secured at the price of truth, it must be recognized, for without reality shared with other human beings, truth loses all meaning. Introspection and its hybrids engender *mendacity*.[15]

But if Rilke's life, with its deliberate ruthlessness toward every relationship that might impinge on his solitary commitment to writing, partially justifies Arendt's strictures against the systematic cultivation of inwardness, the catastrophes of modern European history make clear that neither her idea of "a reality shared with other human beings" nor her motif of a "thinking" that leads directly to "action" can guarantee a beneficent solution to romantic introspection. As both German history and high culture have illustrated, there is no shortage of people eager to validate the most extreme, introspective fantasies of a single, self-proclaimed seer by translating them into collective deeds. The carefully orchestrated, performative inwardness of Hitler's self-representation, what one could call his loneliness on the rostrum, is only the most lethal incarnation of a union of solitary introspection with a will to political leadership that has flourished in the twentieth century as never before.

Obviously Rilke bears no responsibility for the way demagogues subsequently exploited the spell of inwardness that his writings helped nourish, and it is hard to think of an important modern writer more politically uninterested than Rilke. But Arendt's critique of inwardness, like Musil's comment, quoted in the introduction, that "the spiritual veneration of dictators" evident in the careers of artists and thinkers as diverse as Stefan George, Freud, and Karl Kraus preceded the emergence of the century's actual dictators, suggests that there is a relationship among modernism's aesthetic, intellectual, and political currents that is uncomfortably familial and intimate. Even at the strictly personal level, though, it is revelatory to see how fundamental the seductive power of his solitude and inwardness was not only for Rilke's poetry, but also for his erotic life and his important friendships. Many of his most intense love affairs began with a letter from an unknown admirer proclaiming that Rilke's lines seemed to speak directly to her like declarations of a lifelong mutual understanding, and there are numerous moments when the self-abnegation with which some of these correspondents addressed him is distinctly unsettling. Consider, for example, this characteristic declaration by one of these women, the concert pianist Magda von Hattinberg, whom Rilke renamed "Benvenuta," and who, for a few weeks in 1914, became one of the poet's most fervent lovers: "[M]y thoughts acquire purity in you, and no impure thought can exist since it cannot exist in you. The life of the mind for which I have been struggling all these unbearable years . . . that infinite life of the mind, comes true for me in you."[16] Rilke's relationships with others are troubling precisely because they often depend on just this mixture of near servility and unacknowledged self-congratulation that is essential to the worship of a great artist. Since, by definition, the genius's insights are understood to be far beyond the horizon of the vulgar mob, the more deeply one is moved by them, the greater the confirmation of one's own inwardness. Another's inwardness, so the myth insists, can be understood only by an equivalent inwardness of one's own, and to captivate potential lovers and patrons alike, Rilke played upon this belief with all the virtuosity at his command.

There is abundant evidence of Rilke's success in finding an ardent and uninterrupted succession of adherents—or rather in permitting them to find him—and since most of them eventually wrote memoirs about their connection with him, we are more than sufficiently informed today about the vicissitudes of Rilke's erotic history. From important lovers like Lou Andreas-Salomé, Magda von Hattinberg, Loulou Albert-Lasard, and Baladine Klossowska ("Merline"), to his great patron, Princess Marie von Turn und Taxis-Hohenlohe, and from Katharina Kippenberg, the wife of Rilke's publisher at the Insel-Verlag, down to his most casual acquaintances, it sometimes seems as if everyone whose path ever crossed Rilke's has composed an account of the event and published whatever letters she and he exchanged.

There were two notable exceptions to this ritual. One was the sculptor Clara Westhoff (1878–1954), whom Rilke married in 1901 and left shortly thereafter, in order, according to him, to allow them both the freedom to grow as artists. The other was their daughter, Ruth, born seven and a half months after her parents' wedding. Ruth rarely ever saw her father (he did not, for instance, bother to attend her wedding to Carl Sieber in 1922), but until her suicide in 1972, she dedicated her existence to publishing her father's writings and enshrining his memory. Although the bulk of Rilke's letters to Clara and Ruth appear in the published correspondence, neither woman ever produced the kinds of explanatory, self-serving accounts of the poet's character that mark so many of the other memoirs. It is as though they, better than anyone else, had learned the futility of such explanations.

The ready availability of so much intimate biographical material has had the ironic effect of subjecting Rilke, at least posthumously, to the kind of intrusive public scrutiny he most sought to avoid in his lifetime. Nothing mattered so much to him as preserving his privacy and his independence. To do so, he was prepared to break off his most important relationships, not only with women whom he had assiduously courted and whose support he still craved, but also with revered artistic mentors such as Rodin. Yet one of the defining paradoxes of Rilke's legacy is that this poet who deliberately sacrificed himself and those around him to the creation of a monumental, autonomous body of work is now regularly discussed in terms of his most intimate, personal traits.

Rilke's notorious skittishness as a lover, for example, has become a central issue in virtually every recent account of his writing. But in his case, at least, our inquisitiveness is not just another shabby instance of the contemporary, ressentiment-motivated reduction of a great artist to a set of more or less pathological symptoms and politically suspect attitudes. Instead, it is Rilke himself who has made such speculations almost irresistible by so determinedly adopting the rhetoric of a spiritual pilgrim who, through his own painful experiences, has come to understand the true nature of love and who, in turn, therefore, can teach it to his readers.

Rilke's poems contain an astonishing number of imperatives and exhortations. There are no less than *seven* imperatives, for example, in the final "Sonnet to Orpheus," and constructions like "Look: . . . ," "See: . . . ," and "Consider: . . ." are far more common in Rilke than in any of his most notable contemporaries. For a lyric poet of such extraordinary delicacy and indirection, Rilke is also a highly didactic writer. Indeed, his popularity is in part based on his presumed wisdom as a guide to living more authentically. Thus, the impulse to probe the links between the life and the teaching is, in a sense, directly encouraged by Rilke's poetry itself.

In the magnificent elegy written in 1908 after the death of his friend, the painter Paula Modersohn-Becker, Rilke declares:

> Wir haben, wo wir lieben, ja nur dies:
> einander lassen; denn daß wir uns halten,
> das fällt uns leicht und ist nicht erst zu lernen.
> "Requiem: Für eine Freundin"

> We need, in love, to practice only this:
> letting each other go. For holding on
> comes easily; we do not need to learn it.
> "Requiem for a Friend"[17]

Robert Hass, in his introduction to Stephen Mitchell's translations, wryly speculates that Rilke is here "teaching his readers something they probably need to know more than he does."[18] Louise Glück's reaction is simpler and more astringent: she accuses Rilke of "bad faith" in dispensing such advice at all, since "what was hard for *him* was holding on."[19] But this contradiction cannot simply be explained away as a matter of personal bad faith. The dictum that "to love means to be alone" is so utterly central to Rilke's whole sense of human existence that he enunciates it at every stage of his career. The early, and often preposterously pontifical, volume *Letters to a Young Poet* is already full of phrases like "loving, for a long time ahead and far into life, is solitude, a heightened and deepened kind of aloneness."[20] A few years later, in 1910, Rilke sharply condensed these words for his great novel *The Notebooks of Malte Laurids Brigge*, but, it is important to emphasize, without in any way modifying their import: "nothing can be meant by union save increased loneliness."[21] The same insistent note is repeatedly sounded at the very heart of the *Duino Elegies*, from the First Elegy's praise for those whose unrequited love frees them from the paltriness of sexual and emotional possessiveness to the Fourth Elegy's bleak question:

> . . . Treten Liebende
> nicht immerfort an Ränder, eins im andern,
> die sich versprachen Weite, Jagd und Heimat.

> . . . Aren't lovers
> Always arriving at each other's boundaries?
> although they promised vastness, hunting, home.[22]

Finally, in a breathtakingly tender admonition, the *Sonnets to Orpheus* enjoin the renunciation of eros and of life itself, until letting go is understood as the proper response to everything that constrains us to one desire, one form of being:

> Sei allem Abschied voran, als wäre er hinter
> dir, wie der Winter, der eben geht.

> Be ahead of all parting, as though it already were
> behind you, like the winter that has just gone by.[23]

Rilke was certainly always prepared to use these same arguments defensively in order to extricate himself from any relationship that had grown too demanding, and in this regard, Glück's charge of "bad faith" is amply warranted. But to conceive, as Rilke does, something like a plenitude of renunciation, and then to make that plenitude the core of his writing, did not come as readily or painlessly to Rilke as we often assume. The loneliness was as real as the flight from intimacy, and the fear of physical and emotional suffering as great as the constant injunction to see life and death as a single, unbroken continuum.

Rilke was often terrified of his own isolation, and he knew that the loneliness he chose left him exposed to all the turbulence of his emotions without anyone to help alleviate or redirect them. Opening himself to that turbulence was also, of course, the all-important reward of breaking free from the sheltering intimacies of his affairs. But Rilke's writing makes clear that by withdrawing from the solicitude that his lovers offered, he was turning away from something that a part of him deeply craved. He recognizes in himself "an incessant longing to lodge my aloneness with some person, to place it in his protection," and if he was often callously evasive, and even exploitative, in his treatment of others, no one knew that better than Rilke himself.[24] His texts are full of harsh self-criticisms probing the gap between his spiritual insights and the weakness of his own character. His poetry can celebrate the serenity of existing without possessiveness, but, as he regularly tells Lou Andreas-Salomé, Rilke experiences himself as a someone who is "nothing else but desire" who "spoils everything" by the intensity with which he forces his own will and consciousness on everything around him.[25]

The inwardness Rilke sought was sometimes antithetical to simple human intimacy, but also sometimes directly allied to it. Negotiating that precarious balance placed an impossible burden on Rilke's companions, and he himself often floundered amid its confusions. But perhaps nothing is more moving in his descriptions of the transmutation of "loneliness" into concentrative joy than when it occurs amid the most ordinary, prosaic objects and tasks. The "bridge, pitcher, fruit-tree, and window" from the Ninth Elegy are Rilke's equivalent to the terra-cotta milk jug and bowl that Vermeer's servant girl, alone in the kitchen and focused entirely on her task, uses to prepare breakfast. The unity of inwardness and contented solitude amid the fulfillment of quotidian tasks is among Rilke's central poetic achievements, and one in which his only real peers are Vermeer and Emily Dickinson. But in other texts of desolate loneliness, such as *The Notebooks of Malte Laurids Brigge*, Rilke could crystallize a different kind of isolated inwardness altogether: a deadening, bleak, and almost vacant inner emptiness that is only intensified by being echoed and shared by everyone nearby. If one might think of the first state as a kind of affirmative, Vermeer-like solitude, the second could be called the Edward Hopper–like loneliness of pure disconnection.[26] To have been able to find a language for both these moments of consciousness and mood is, I think, unique to Rilke and accounts for why readers continue to turn to him long after many of his vatic poses have lost their appeal.

The evidence of his voluminous correspondence and the extensive accounts of those who knew him, alongside the almost hierophantic claims implicit in his own often moralizing exhortations, make the question of ethical judgment particularly difficult to avoid in Rilke's case. This is especially true because the basic outline of Rilke's life has already been told so many times and turned into so potent a parable—most effectively by Rilke himself in numerous well-known letters and stories. Parables have their own inexorable logic, and Rilke was determined to make his life into a narratable, coherent plot. In this, he was spectacularly successful. Virtually every phase of his existence now has its own monographs, and there are numerous richly detailed biographies, both scholarly and anecdotal, to provide interested readers with almost week-by-week accounts of Rilke's activities, contacts, and reflections. Nonetheless, after reading enough of these studies, it is hard not to think longingly of Auden's famous line, "A shilling life will give you all the facts."[27]

Rilke's life was so entirely focused on his writing that the facts really can be— and often have been—summarized perfectly adequately in a few pages. Indeed, the events of Rilke's life have come to form the indispensable framework for an elaborately scripted legend. From his birth in Prague on December 4, 1875, to middle-class parents who were utterly ill suited to one another and soon separated, to his death in Switzerland fifty-one years later of an excruciatingly painful form of leukemia, every important event in Rilke's life has been retrospectively endowed with the aura of an ineluctable destiny.

His more devoted readers can enumerate the handful of emblematic incidents with the same intensity and inwardness that they bring to their recitation of "Autumn Day," and in all such accounts certain details are regarded as decisive. At birth, he was given the sexually ambiguous name "René Maria," and his mother kept him in girl's clothes until he was seven. (Not until he had turned twenty-two did Lou Andreas-Salomé persuade him to adopt the more Germanically masculine "Rainer.") In 1886, however, his mother's unwelcome cosseting was replaced by the harshness of military boarding schools, including a period in Mährisch-Weißkirchen, the same academy in Moravia that Robert Musil had so loathed when he was a pupil there a few years earlier and which he subsequently used as the setting for his first novel, Young Törless. Almost immediately after being expelled from Mährisch-Weißkirchen in 1891, Rilke began to devote himself with increasing tenacity to becoming a great poet. From then on, everything would be subordinated to that all-consuming task.

In a sense, his real biography consists of only three significant categories: first, and most important, the list of books he published, beginning in 1894 with the painfully immature Life and Song and ending in 1926, six months before his death, with Vergers, suivi des Quatrains Valaisans, a collection of poems written in French; second, the women he loved and the very few men with whom he established a lasting connection; and third, the many places he visited or lived in, including, especially, the north German artist colony of Worpswede, where he met Clara Westhoff and Paula Becker, the two trips to Russia with Lou Andreas-Salomé, the decisive, prolonged residence in Paris, the retreat to the castle at Duino, near Trieste, where he began his major composition, the Duino Elegies in 1912, and his stay in Muzot, Switzerland, where, in 1923, he finally completed the Elegies and the Sonnets to Orpheus.

This catalog of dates, names, and places may seem uninspiring as the material of myth, but in Rilke's case, each detail has been burnished and refined to fit perfectly into the master narrative of his life as a painful but ultimately triumphant quest. Like a fairy tale or folk legend, this quest, too, has been endowed with its own elegantly simple and comprehensive unities: there are four distinct stages, each punctuated by a dramatic upheaval. The first phase, from 1875 to 1902, represents his apprentice years. It covers Rilke from his childhood until the move to Paris and includes not only the all-important first encounter with Lou Andreas-Salomé, but also his marriage to Clara Westhoff, and the beginning of a real, if still limited, reputation as a poet. The second interval marks the difficult transition from discipleship to mastery. It extends from 1902 until 1912 and is triggered by Rilke's acute dissatisfaction with his early writing, his search for a way to radically transform his poetics, and his flight from the constraints of fatherhood and domesticity. The turbulent apprenticeship to Rodin, the establishing of lifelong bonds with his principal patrons, and several of his most significant love affairs took place during these years. Most important, though, these were the years that Rilke published a series of major works, including such masterpieces as the two parts of *New Poems*, the "Requiem for a Friend," and his novel, *The Notebooks of Malte Laurids Brigge*. By 1910, Rilke's fame as one of the preeminent German poets of the age was secure. But then, early in 1912, during an extended stay at Duino Castle, the indispensable central event of the whole legend occurred. It is worth quoting extensively from Princess Marie von Thurn und Taxis-Hohenlohe's account of that defining moment, since her version, in all its romantic grandiloquence, has assumed canonical status in the Rilke myth:

> Then, one morning, he received a troublesome business letter. He wanted to take care of it quickly. . . . Outside, a violent north wind was blowing, but the sun shone and the water gleamed as if covered with silver. Rilke climbed down to the bastions which . . . were connected to the foot of the castle by a narrow path along the cliffs, which abruptly drop off, for about two hundred feet, into the sea. Rilke walked back and forth, completely absorbed in the problem of how to answer the letter. Then, all at once, in the midst of his thoughts, he stopped; it seemed that from the raging storm a voice had called to him, "Who, if I cried out, would hear me among the angels' hierarchies?" He stood still, listening. "What is that?" he whispered. "What is it, what is coming?" Taking out the notebook that he always carried with him, he wrote down these words, together with a few lines that formed by themselves without his intervention. Who was coming? . . . He knew it now: [it was] the God. . . .
>
> Very calmly he climbed back up to his room, set his notebook aside, and answered the difficult letter. By the evening the whole First Elegy had been written.[28]

During the succeeding days, Rilke went on to write the Second, much of the Third, and scattered lines of what later became the Sixth, Ninth, and Tenth Elegies, before the inspiration stopped as quickly as it had seized him. A longing for the return of that revelation, and for the "gift" of being able to complete the Elegies, is what fills the next decade from 1912 to 1922, a span that, in this schema, is invariably seen as a barren wilderness in which Rilke did nothing but wait for the sense of emptiness to be lifted from him. The cataclysm of World War I, Rilke's successful effort to avoid frontline service in the Imperial Habsburg army, the postwar confusion of Munich, and the move to Switzerland in 1919 are all secondary to the poet's restlessness and depression as he waited for a second "Duino experience."

As in all successful quest stories there is a final, triumphant phase. In the Rilke legend, this phase occurs between 1921 and 1926, and it begins when Rilke takes up residence in the small château of Muzot where he will miraculously be granted the gift of fulfilling his life's work. In February 1922, during two weeks of unmatched productivity and inspiration, he completed not only the *Duino Elegies*, but also all fifty-five *Sonnets to Orpheus*. Thereafter, even though he kept on composing new works, including a series of translations of Valéry, Rilke's mission was essentially at an end. Combined with what he had already written, this astonishing late output had made him indisputably the greatest German poet since Hölderlin. His pain-racked death in 1926 was not so much the cutting off of a career, but more a kind of belated crossing-over into what he had always regarded as another, equally valid order of being.

Or so, at least, the legend would have it. And for all its heavy-handed, mono-lithic emplotment, this is the model to which all the major biographies more or less strictly adhere. But there is ample evidence to suggest a considerably more complex and nuanced story. Initially, there is the curious matter of how conscientiously Rilke managed his career, how careful he was to mail fulsomely inscribed copies of his early publications to the major writers of the day, even including such unlikely figures as the much older, realistic novelist, Theodor Fontane (1819–98). Indeed, Rilke's biographers make clear that as his fame increased, "he reserved relatively few [copies of new books] for old friends in Prague," preferring to cultivate "new contacts" in Munich and the wider German literary world.[29] In themselves, Rilke's careerism and his artful courting of a series of increasingly prominent patrons are not in the least disreputable, but they sit uneasily with his reputation for unworldly inwardness.

Far more tellingly, though, there is a great deal that is false about the whole formulaic schema according to which his life is narrated. The terms in which Rilke chose to make sense of his existence are often in conflict with his actual accomplishments, and it is surprising for how long and how uncritically those terms have been adopted by his interpreters. Instead of passively enduring the long fallow periods that represent the melancholic corollaries to his bursts of visionary realizations, Rilke actually composed constantly, and often at the highest level, during the years he was supposedly doing little except waiting for another revelation from the "Angel of Duino." Edward Snow's introduction to his fine translation of Rilke's *Uncollected Poems* makes this point particularly well, and he rightly blames the relative obscurity of these texts on "the ever-present myth of Rilke's *Duino* crisis, and that myth's way of obscuring whatever might contradict it or undermine its drama."[30] Rilke was the first and most important creator of his own legend, and after 1912, he was committed to seeing his life's "true task" as the completion of the *Duino Elegies*. All else was merely secondary, more like finger exercises than real creation. So powerful has this myth become that it was allowed to determine crucial bibliographic and textual decisions about how to edit his work, thereby further obscuring his actual accomplishments. The enormous prestige of the standard, six-volume German edition of Rilke's *Collected Works* has always worked to validate the most conventional narrative of the poet's career, and, as Snow rightly insists, its canonical division of Rilke's texts into separate sections labeled "completed works" (*Vollendetes*), "dedications" (*Widmungen*), and "drafts" (*Entwürfe*) "makes it impossible to experience the poems in their temporal succession and imposes on them the very distinctions they so curiously blur."[31]

As soon as one discards the arbitrary arrangement of the *Collected Works* and reads the poems in chronological order, the range and the uninterrupted fluency of Rilke's productivity becomes startlingly clear. Alongside such unmistakably major achievements as "The Spanish Trilogy," "The Raising of Lazarus," and "The Spirit Ariel," all written within days of one another early in 1913 (supposedly one of Rilke's "sterile" and "uninspired" periods), there are brief lyrics of such quiet, yearning tenderness that it is impossible to read them and still believe that "letting go" of love always came so easily to him:

> Denn ich *gedenke* nicht, das, was ich *bin*
> rührt mich um deinetwillen. Ich erfinde
> dich nicht an traurig ausgekühlten Stellen,
> von wo du wegkamst; selbst, daß du nicht da bist,
> ist warm von dir und wirklicher und mehr
> als ein Entbehren . . .
> > "An Lou Andreas-Salomé, III"

> For I don't *think back;* all that I *am*
> stirs me because of you. I don't invent you
> at sadly cooled-off places from which
> you've gone away; even your not being there
> is warm with you and more real and more
> than a privation . . .
> > "To Lou Andreas-Salomé"[32]

Well after the completion of the *Duino Elegies* and the *Sonnets to Orpheus*, Rilke kept composing wonderfully fresh poems whose clarities are closer to the best of the 1906 *Book of Images* than to the two great volumes that are usually allowed to define his final years. A poem such as "Early Spring," written in February 1924, marvelously combines the rhythmic subtleties and unexpected shifts of imagery of the *Elegies* and *Sonnets* with the intense absorption in a simple landscape of Rilke's Worpswede period:

Härte schwand. Auf einmal legt sich Schonung
an der Wiesen aufgedecktes Grau.
Kleine Wasser ändern die Betonung.
Zärtlichkeiten, ungenau,

greifen nach der Erde aus dem Raum.
Wege gehen weit ins Land und zeigens.
Unvermutet siehst du seines Steigens
Ausdruck in dem leeren Baum.

"Vorfrühling"

Harshness disappeared. Suddenly caring spreads itself
on the field's uncovered gray.
Small rivulets change their intonations.
Tendernesses, inexpertly,

reach toward the earth from space.
Roads run far into the land, foretelling it.
Unexpectedly you see its rising's
visage in the empty tree.

"Early Spring"[33]

For all the indisputable gains that he made over the years in technique, there is far more continuity between the early and late poems than most of his readers, or perhaps even Rilke himself, recognized. What one might call the non-Orphic side of Rilke's voice flourishes in these uncollected poems as nowhere else in his mature verse, and yet they, too, contain the same kinds of deeply unsettling strangeness as do the canonic major texts. The evidence of these poems, alongside a more skeptical interpretation of the readily available biographical information, should finally let us get beyond the simplifications of the canonic Rilke legend with its dreary cycles of transcendent inspiration and imaginative paralysis. By now, such a demystification is an essential first step toward a more genuinely responsive—and responsible—reading of the poetry itself.

In her journal on October 5, 1913, Lou Andreas-Salomé noted that for Rilke poetry was "all a release into himself and not a form of communication."[34] As usual, she is Rilke's shrewdest observer. Yet paradoxically, that uncommunicative "release into himself" has communicated more intensely to readers than the words of any other modern German-language poet. Even in English, which is notoriously inimical to many of Rilke's resources, a surprising amount of his power comes through. He can give abstract substantives like Being or Aloneness all the solidity of concrete, tangible objects, and make his ideas as sensuously immediate and physically tangible as William Carlos Williams's red wheelbarrow and white chickens.

Admittedly, the densely compacted word formations and the neologisms that are possible in German, and for which Rilke, along with Paul Celan, had an unparalleled gift, are part of what make a line like this from the *Sonnets to Orpheus*, "Sei—und wisse zugleich des Nicht-Seins Bedingung," absolutely typical of Rilke and utterly resistant to translation (literally: Be—and know at the same time Not-Being's Requirement).[35] Neither Stephen Mitchell's California Zen rendering, "Be—and yet know the great void where all things begin," nor C. F. MacIntyre's impossibly abstruse interpretation, "Be—at the same time, know the terms of negation," succeeds in making Rilke's line remotely persuasive as English verse. The odd combination of prosiness and abstraction in A. Poulin's version, "Be—and at the same time know the implications/of non-being," is closer to Rilke's meaning, but it lacks all of his forcefulness and rhythmic assurance. It is worth noting, though, that even for German-language readers, the line is tremendously hard to grasp with anything like a reliably paraphrasable meaning. Yet even in English, the sonnet from which the line is taken, with its haunting initial imperative, "Be ahead of all parting," survives its denaturing to remain one of the most cherished texts of the whole cycle.

> Sei allem Abschied voran, als wäre er hinter
> dir, wie der Winter, der eben geht.
> Denn unter Wintern ist einer so endlos Winter,
> daß, überwinternd, dein Herz überhaupt übersteht.

> Be ahead of all parting, as though it already were
> behind you, like the winter that has just gone by.
> For among these winters there is one so endlessly winter
> that only by wintering through it will your heart survive.[36]

Rilke's inwardness intrigues and moves readers so powerfully, even when it reaches them in a language whose strengths are so alien to that of his own, largely because it speaks from a view of the self that confronts the most fundamental questions of life, desire, and mortality without drawing on any of the leveling tropes or dubious scientisms of traditional psychology. This is also why biographies of Rilke are usually so unsatisfying: they can tell us nothing about inwardness because it is fundamentally neither a narrative nor a psychological category at all. Rilke's inwardness is the absolute antithesis to any form of normative psychology, just as his ideas of love as endless leave-taking go against every conventional notion of intimacy. Like Freud, Rilke used his own fears, illnesses, and neuroses as the foundation for a theory of what it means to be fully "at home" in the world, but his sense of what that entails is at once more inclusive and less dogmatic than Freud's. Perhaps this is why Lou Andreas-Salomé, although herself one of Freud's earliest disciples and the author of numerous significant psychoanalytic writings, recommended against Rilke's ever going into analysis.

It is not the specific tenets of his personal metaphysics, but rather Rilke's whole language and tone, his basic way of framing questions, that implies an immensely suggestive alternative to any psychoanalytic idea of the self. It begins, as any persuasive alternative must, with a deep respect for the ultimate impenetrability of the human heart:

> . . . Wir kennen den Kontur
> des Fühlens nicht: nur, was ihn formt von außen.
>> Wer saß nicht bang vor seines Herzens Vorhang?
> Der schlug sich auf: die Szenerie war Abschied.
>>> "Die vierte Elegie"

> . . . we never know
> the actual, vital contour of our own
> emotions—just what forms them from outside.
>> Who has not sat, afraid, before his heart's
> curtain? It rose: the scenery of farewell.
>>> Fourth Elegy[37]

Rilke profoundly respected his own privacy. He was, in a manner already rare in his own day, decorous toward himself, and his style of decorousness did not require any sacrifice of strictness or lucidity. He thus offered his readers a way to find a correspondingly lucid decorum toward themselves and their own psyches. The very idiosyncrasy of Rilke's language, with its haunting and immediately recognizable word coinings and images, is a way of safeguarding the radical specificity of individual experience from any homogenizing discourse, whether psychological, political, or conventionally religious. Despite his occasionally vatic posturing, Rilke's poetry would never be as rich if it contained just monuments to his own inwardness or a set of universalizing explanations on which yet another master system could be erected. At its best, Rilke's verse shows us how to heed our own interior speech, and to heed it, surprisingly enough, without the overwrought intensities of psychoanalytic narratives.

What continues to resonate most deeply in Rilke's work is not just the unmixed high rhetoric of his "inspired" set pieces, but rather a totally unexpected union of simplicity and transcendence expressed in a tone that shifts with complete naturalness from the prosaic to the cosmic:

. . . Wie Tau von dem Frühgras
hebt sich das Unsre von uns, wie die Hitze von einem
heißen Gericht . . .
    . . . Schmeckt denn der Weltraum,
in den wir uns lösen, nach uns?

"Die zweite Elegie"

    . . . Like dew from the morning grass,
what is ours floats into the air, like steam from a dish
of hot food . . .
        Does the infinite space
we dissolve into, taste of us then?

Second Elegy[38]

Time after time in his later writings, Rilke seems to come upon and name his own inwardness not like the expression of an already known and permanently assured possession, but like a sudden discovery, a gift accepted in a spirit that contains both gratitude and an objective assessment of its lineaments. The real weakness of the early volumes was that their yearning so often remained purely self-referential: affirmations of a desire that had no object beyond itself. Even the moments of despair had too much mere self-display. It is impossible to date the extraordinary change in Rilke with any precision, but its consequences are unmistakable. In a poem from 1913 he speaks of "Innigstes unser" (innermost thing of ours) as that which "exceeds us," and acknowledges that in order to know what is within, a person must reach a moment

        da uns das Innre umsteht
        als geübteste Ferne, als andre
        Seite der Luft . . .
                "An die Musik"

        when the inner surrounds us
        as the most practiced distance, as the air's
        other side . . .
                    "To Music"[39]

Rilke's sense of what inwardness has come to mean to him can articulate itself only through this play of contradictory affirmations. His lines marshal a responsiveness that must be directed equally to what is wholly interior and what feels furthest away and most inhospitable. The inner and the external both mirror and mutually guarantee one another's existence for Rilke, and their interdependence is precisely what grounds Rilke's mature poetics. One of Simone Weil's great aphorisms from *Gravity and Grace* says that "the virtue of humility is nothing more nor less than the power of attention."[40] Somehow, by teaching himself how to focus with such unwavering attentiveness on the world of external objects and created things, Rilke was able to fashion not just a new poetic language for moments of heightened perception, but also, and more uncannily, a radically fresh way of understanding and experiencing his own inner life. Subjectivity became the greatest prize of his objectivity. He came to say "I" the way he said "house, bridge, fountain . . . ," and for the same numinous, unsentimental ends. Listen, simply, to the way he can weave consolation out of the joining of personal sorrow to the rush of stellar spaces without denying the reality of either, or just turning one into only a metaphor of the other:

> Überfließende Himmel verschwendeter Sterne
> prachten über der Kümmernis. Statt in die Kissen,
> weine hinauf. Hier, an dem weinenden schon,
> an dem endenden Antlitz,
> um sich greifend, beginnt der hin-
> reißende Weltraum. Wer unterbricht,
> wenn du dort hin drängst,
> die Strömung? Keiner. Es sei denn,
> daß du plötzlich ringst mit der gewaltigen Richtung
> jener Gestirne nach dir. Atme.
> Atme das Dunkel der Erde und wieder
> aufschau! Wieder. Leicht und gesichtlos
> lehnt sich von oben Tiefe dir an. Das gelöste
> nachtenthaltne Gesicht giebt dem deinigen Raum.
>   "Überfließende Himmel verschwendeter Sterne"

> Overflowing heavens of squandered stars
> flame brilliantly above your troubles. Instead
> of onto your pillows, weep up toward them.
> There, at the already weeping, at the ending visage,
> slowly thinning out, ravishing
> worldspace begins. Who will interrupt,
> once you've forced your way there,
> the current? No one. You may panic,
> and fight that overwhelming course of stars
> that streams toward you. Breathe.
> Breathe the darkness of the earth and again
> look up! Again. Lightly and facelessly

depths lean toward you from above. The serene
countenance dissolved into night makes room for yours.
"Overflowing heavens"[41]

There have been fewer such transformations of our common terms of self-perception than the standard cultural histories like to pretend. And when Musil linked Rilke to the medieval poets, he must have meant that Rilke's poetry, like theirs, had been among the very few to have shown him authentic glimpses of a different, less possessive relationship to one's inner being, one's desires and one's world. Like the best medieval poets, Rilke often presents his visionary moments through the simplest, most domestic of images. The naive metaphors from the realm of "heaven and heath and house" that once carried so little charge in *The Book of Monastic Life* do more than merely survive into the late poetry; the complexity of their new contexts transforms and enriches them immeasurably, but they in turn bring, even to the oracular insights of the *Duino Elegies*, the indispensable directness of the very greatest art.

At the end, in another of the marvelous late poems written after the *Elegies*, Rilke returns to the one, insistent question he had asked since his earliest writings, but now he is able to answer it with a naturalness of tone that took a lifetime's artistry to master:

> Innres, was ists?
> Wenn nicht gesteigerter Himmel,
> durchworfen mit Vögeln und tief
> von Winden der Heimkehr.
>> "Ach, nicht getrennt sein"

> What is inwardness?
> What if not sky intensified,
> flung through with birds and deep
> with winds of homecoming?
>> "Ah, not to be cut off"[42]

2

Robert Musil
Precision and Soul

W hen Robert Musil died in exile in Geneva on April 15, 1942, he was virtually a forgotten figure, his reputation fading even among his fellow refugees from Nazism, and his masterpiece, *The Man without Qualities* (*Der Mann ohne Eigenschaften*),[1] on which he had labored for over twenty-five years, nowhere near completion. Only eight people attended his cremation, and except for a few scattered and laconic notices, the literary world ignored the event completely.

This lack of attention was not simply a natural consequence of the war's all consuming hold on the imagination, in comparison with which the fate of one individual author could scarcely be expected to arouse much interest. Fifteen months earlier, for instance, James Joyce's death in Zurich was marked by an outpouring of articles in mass-circulation newspapers as well as in literary journals. Moreover, even after the defeat of the Third Reich had restored a German-speaking readership to other émigré authors like Thomas Mann and Bertolt Brecht, Musil remained largely unread and unpublished. Many of his most important texts were published only posthumously, and the first postwar edition of *The Man without Qualities* did not appear until 1952. It took another decade and a half before his works began to be widely translated and anything resembling a consensus about his importance as one of the preeminent European writers of the century emerged.

Today, though, there is little doubt that Musil belongs in the great constellation of novelists like Joyce, Proust, and Kafka, writers who both redefined the formal possibilities of their medium and, in the process, reshaped the ways we use storytelling to make sense of our experience. *The Man without Qualities* is now regularly ransacked for its striking epigraphs and historical aperçus, and it is routinely invoked as one of the especially revelatory documents that nourish our ongoing fascination with the final days of the Austro-Hungarian Empire. But we are still only beginning to comprehend the scrupulous lucidity with which Musil transformed the well-made European novel into an open-ended thought experiment, a "testing ground" for problems whose pertinence is no less powerful today than when he was writing. The reaction of even a generally sympathetic critic like J. P. Stern is typical of the deep-seated ambivalence that Musil's formal, as well as thematic, originality continues to arouse: "To the question whether what he has written is a great novel there is, I think, only one answer: it is great, but it is not a novel."[2] Clearly, then, if the recognition of Musil's mastery has taken so long to secure, this is not due merely to resistance against the intrinsic difficulty of his work. Instead, the whole nature of his achievement, the ways in which his work is both difficult and rewarding, constitutes so singular a case that even a thorough grounding—and delight—in the complexities of the other great modernist authors does little to prepare one for an encounter with a body of writing like his.

It is his unprecedented combination of eroticism and rationality, mysticism and scientific rigor that distinguishes Musil from even the most brilliant of his contemporaries. Like many thinkers in the first third of the twentieth century, Musil was tormented by the sense that modern consciousness was becoming increasingly splintered and fragmentary, lacking the kind of central, synthesizing principles that could command the simultaneous allegiance of mind and heart. In the lapidary formulation of one of his *Diary* entries, "The facts of contemporary life have outgrown the concepts of the old."[3] But in an epoch when thinking itself was becoming ferociously politicized and ideological, Musil had only contempt for the catastrophic simplifications of totalitarian movements, whether they came from the left or the right wing. Nor did a purely aesthetic solution hold any appeal for him; he never aimed just to create another significant work of art, but rather to use all the resources of both his scientific training and his literary imagination to find a way out of the sterile oppositions of his era. Musil kept looking for a way to make sense of himself and the world that would not be compartmentalized into discrete domains. The new ethical, moral, and sexual dispensation he sought would have to reflect the scientific, practical world modern men and women inhabit, but also be able to overcome its isolating and dehumanizing effects.

The decisive initial difference between Musil and most of the other modernist literary masters is the fact that he came to literature from science and demanded from his own fiction the intellectual rigor and precision that he had learned in the laboratory. He was a true polymath, as expert in theoretical physics, experimental psychology, and mechanical engineering as in strictly literary or philosophical questions. The prewar Austrian intelligentsia placed a much higher value on a rigorous scientific education than did their counterparts in England, France, or the United States. One need think only of Ludwig Wittgenstein, who was initially trained in mechanical engineering and first came to England in 1908 to study aeronautics at Manchester before finally turning to philosophy relatively late in his education. Like Wittgenstein, but far more understanding of the vicissitudes of sexual desire, Musil sought throughout his whole life to combine a commitment to the most stringent principles of mathematical logic with a mystical yearning for a new, less alienated way of living. Musil despised the widespread habit of substituting a grandiloquently soulful rhetoric for the kind of disciplined intellectual labor that understanding oneself and the world requires. "Anyone who is incapable of solving an integral equation, anyone who is unable to perform a laboratory experiment, should today be forbidden to discuss all spiritual matters" is a characteristically pugnacious formulation in Musil's play *The Enthusiasts* (*Die Schwärmer*) [4] And in his principal work, *The Man without Qualities*, the conventional insistence that true inwardness is incompatible with logical rigor is one of the reasons that Ulrich, the book's eponymous hero, was first attracted to the hard sciences: "one thing . . . could safely be said about Ulrich: he loved mathematics because of the kind of people who could not endure it."[5] So when Diotima, the novel's society hostess, discovers to her delight that she has a profoundly yearning soul, the narrator mordantly comments on such self-serving pretensions to spiritual inwardness: "What is a soul? It is easy to define negatively: It is simply that which sneaks off at the mention of algebraic series."[6]

Musil's early preparation for his quest to unite mathematics and mysticism was as idiosyncratic as the project itself. He was born in Klagenfurt, Carinthia, in 1880, the son of a gifted, hardworking, and emotionally distant civil engineer with a distinguished career in academic and administrative appointments, and a mother whose temperament was flamboyantly sexual and self-dramatizing. In 1882, when Musil's mother openly took a lover, Heinrich Reiter, her husband seems to have accepted the situation without a struggle, and in 1890 Reiter accompanied the Musil family as their regular "house guest" to Brünn (Brno), where Alfred Musil moved to become professor of mechanical engineering. This permanent and oddly domestic ménage à trois lasted without any serious disruptions until Hermine Musil's death in 1924. Although an outstanding student, Robert suffered from severe attacks of nerves throughout his childhood, and biographers have speculated, often based only on the ambiguous evidence of his fiction, about the links between his recurrent emotional crises and his family's eccentric sexual configuration. What is indisputable, though, and perhaps even stranger, is how Musil was haunted by the image of his "lost" sister, Elsa, who died, at less than eleven months old, four years before his own birth. The motif of a vanished and then rediscovered sister, a twin with whom all intimacy is possible but at the risk of transgressing into the illicit and demonic, became central to *The Man without Qualities*. The most moving relationship in the novel, indeed the only one whose potential the book takes seriously, is the sexually charged affinity between Ulrich and his sister, Agathe, siblings "who are doppelgängers, who have two souls, but are one."[7] Their mutual attachment is characterized by Agathe herself, with only the faintest trace of the normal Musilian irony, as "no longer a love story; it is the very last love story there can be."[8]

Like many boys of his social class, Musil was sent to boarding schools as an adolescent. For three years he attended the famous cadet institution in Mährisch-Weißkirchen, and although he was only somewhat happier there than Rilke had been a few years earlier, Musil was able to draw on his experiences at the school for his first significant writing. *Young Törless*, Musil's first novel, was published to considerable critical acclaim in 1906 and contains a bitter account of the boarding school's atmosphere of claustrophobia, snobbism, homosexual brutality, and intellectual nullity. He abandoned his plans for a military career in 1898, after just one year in Vienna at the Military Academy of Technology, and returned to Brünn to take up civil engineering. Once back in Brünn, though, he also began to attend lectures on literature and philosophy, and he became more systematic about noting down his personal impressions and projects in a series of diaries that he continued to keep for the rest of his life. In 1902 he obtained an assistantship at Germany's most advanced laboratory for mechanical engineering, the Technical Institute in Stuttgart, but a year later, he was already bored with his research and moved to Berlin to begin doctoral studies in philosophy (particularly logic) and experimental psychology. Musil continued to read widely in literature, while simultaneously applying his engineering skills to patent a new design for a color wheel used in experimental psychology tests. In Berlin, Musil studied with Carl Stumpf (to whom Edmund Husserl later dedicated his *Logical Investigations*), and in 1908 he received his doctorate in philosophy, physics, and mathematics for a thesis on Ernst Mach, the Austrian physicist and philosopher for whom the Mach number, representing the ratio of the speed of an object to the speed of sound in the atmosphere, was named.

But to the disgruntlement of his family, which was still supporting him financially, Musil rejected the academic post that he was offered in Graz in order to devote himself entirely to writing. In 1911, he married Martha Marcovaldi, née Heimann (1874–1949), a Jewish-born Berliner who had been married twice before and was seven years his elder. Martha had been trained as a visual artist, and her studies had included classes at a school founded by Lovis Corinth. She became the one indispensable partner on whom Musil would rely, both for his writing and his emotional well-being. Although Agathe in *The Man without Qualities* differs in many ways from Martha Musil, it is fascinating to see how often Musil referred to his wife as his "married sister." The short stories he was writing during these years, "The Perfecting of a Love" and "The Temptation of Quiet Veronica," seem almost collaborative works, so clearly can one sense the perspective and voice of Martha in the texture of both narratives. Indeed, Musil, along with Joyce, is one of the few important modern novelists to have made eroticism in marriage a central part of his reflective preoccupations. Despite Musil's initial literary success, however, his refusal of an academic career left the couple in precarious circumstances throughout his life, and neither his regular work as a reviewer, an editor, and a cultural critic for leading journals in Berlin and Vienna, nor his brief stints at the Library of the Technical University in Vienna (1911–14) and at the Press Office of the Austrian Foreign Ministry (1919–20), assured him any financial stability. Musil served with distinction throughout the First World War in some of the harshest conditions the Imperial Army faced, but when he returned to civilian life, his long-term prospects were even less secure than they had been in 1914. In *The Man without Qualities*, Ulrich has sufficient means to take off a year from his work as a mathematician in order to live free of external constraints, and there is no doubt that his fictional hero's economic independence represents the wish fulfillment of Musil's own unrealized longings.

Musil continued to publish essays in both Germany and Austria on an enormous range of topics, including politics, art, cinema, metaphysics, and the nature of essayistic thinking. The best of these—they are available in English as *Precision and Soul*—contain some of the century's most searching discussions of the breakdown of the European intellectual and imaginative order. Sentences like "We do not have too much intellect and too little soul, but too little intellect in matters of the soul" (from "Helpless Europe")[9] and "If I want to have a worldview, then I must view the world" (from "The German as Symptom")[10] are gradually becoming as much a part of the German aphoristic tradition as the most memorable of Nietzsche's and Schopenhauer's epigrams. But even the relative success of his two plays, *The Enthusiasts*, published in 1921, and the still-untranslated *Vincent and the Mistress of Important Men* (*Vinzenz und die Freundin bedeutender Männer*), which appeared in 1923, did little to improve his financial position. The need for a steady income became all the more pressing as Musil began to devote himself with ever increasing determination to his great novel. Musil's diary entries show that elements of *The Man without Qualities* began to crystallize in his mind well before the outbreak of World War I. By 1919 he had already blocked out many of the book's fundamental themes and specific situations, and by 1924 he was working on it full time.

Beginning in 1925, Musil was receiving regular, if modest, advances for the novel (still tentatively called "The Twin Sister") from his publisher, Ernst Rowohlt, and in 1926 Musil gave the first extensive interview in a literary journal about his forthcoming book. In October 1930, at the urging of the increasingly impatient Rowohlt, Musil published the first volume of *The Man without Qualities*, 1,075 pages containing all of parts 1 and 2 ("A Sort of Introduction" and "Pseudoreality Prevails"). In 1933, again yielding to pressure from Rowohlt, Musil reluctantly published a second volume of 608 pages, comprising a portion of part 3 ("Into the Millennium" ["The Criminals"]). Musil strongly resented having to publish his work piecemeal. He was afraid that once a significant portion was in print, he would be locked into formulations and character descriptions that did not fully satisfy him, without having the chance to revise these parts in the light of subsequent realizations. Since he regarded his novel as a kind of experiment in progress, he was as reluctant to publish his "results" prematurely as he would have been to circulate an early draft of a paper in mathematics or logic.

At almost the same time as the second volume appeared, Robert and Martha left Berlin for Vienna, appalled by Hitler's accession to power. After the Nazi annexation of Austria in 1938, the Musils again fled, this time to Switzerland, where they lived on increasingly depleted resources until the writer's death in 1942. A third volume of *The Man without Qualities* had been prepared by Musil for publication in 1938, in an effort to keep alive some public interest in his work. The book contained twenty chapters intended as a continuation of part 3, not as its conclusion, but Musil withdrew them when they were already set in galleys. No further parts of *The Man without Qualities* appeared during Musil's lifetime, but in 1943 Martha had the withdrawn chapters, along with a very small selection from his voluminous drafts and fragments, published at her own expense in Lausanne as volume 3. Since 1952, under the editorship of Adolf Frisé, who had become fascinated with Musil's novel in the 1930s and contacted Martha after the war to inquire about the state of the manuscripts, *The Man without Qualities* has appeared in increasingly expanded and revised editions, incorporating more of Musil's posthumous fragments and draft chapters (the *Nachlaß*). The latest of these editions was published in 1978 and serves as the basis of the 1995 English translation by Sophie Wilkins and Burton Pike, but almost everything about the *Nachlaß*, from the internal order of the chapters to their degree of relative completeness, remains conjectural, and every new edition has occasioned fierce and often highly technical controversies in which vital interpretative, as well as purely bibliographic, issues are at stake. Like the narrative of *The Man without Qualities*, the physical book itself, as a material product, turns out to have remained open-ended and subject to limitless revision.

More than most long and complex novels, *The Man without Qualities* resists being summarized. Far from coming together to form a coherent plot, the book's diverse incidents become increasingly more disparate and fragmented as the novel unfolds. Indeed, the inability of separate stories, motifs, and perspectives to coalesce into a meaningful pattern is one of Musil's major themes. *The Man without Qualities* may be understood as a series of events in search of a plot, just as the Habsburg Empire itself is shown as a haphazard political amalgam engaged in a hopeless search for some unifying meaning or identity.

At the center of all these stories, and providing the novel's sustained focus and source of continuity, is Ulrich, the "man without qualities." An ex-soldier, an experimental scientist, a brilliant mathematician, and a casual womanizer, Ulrich decides, at the age of thirty-two, to take a yearlong "vacation from life" so as to discover in himself the intellectual rigor, spiritual intensity, and emotional depth that, he has grown to feel, must underlie any meaningful action. He has many talents, but he has no qualities, in the sense that his acute self-awareness detaches him from his own attributes and gives them, in his eyes, a kind of impersonal and even transitory nature. If the other characters in the book have a stable identity and the conviction that whatever belief system bolsters their position in the world must be universally beneficent, Ulrich deliberately resists the reassurance of such stability; he does not want to assume a possessive stance toward the qualities he has, nor use them to take a proprietary attitude toward the world. Everyone in the novel is certain both *how* to think and *what* truly merits being thought about except Ulrich, who is certain about neither.

The Man without Qualities opens in August 1913, less than a year before the assassination of Franz Ferdinand, the presumptive heir to the Habsburg throne, triggered the outbreak of the First World War. The specific historical situation is central to the novel's unfolding, since Ulrich is prodded by his anxious father, a judge with aristocratic connections, and by his beautiful, ambitious cousin, Ermelinde Tuzzi (nicknamed "Diotima"),[11] to assume the position of secretary for a grandiose but incoherent plan—the Parallel Campaign (*Parallelaktion*)—to celebrate the seventieth anniversary of Emperor Franz Joseph's coronation, which is due to fall on December 2, 1918. Conceived as a patriotic response to the already formulated German idea of honoring their monarch, Wilhelm II, on July 15, 1918, with a national festival celebrating his thirty years on the throne, the Austrian scheme is pathetically, even risibly, futile, since Franz Joseph was to die in 1916, and in 1918 both the Austrian and the German empires would collapse and be replaced by republics. The only "parallel action" that will actually take place is the almost simultaneous downfall of both dynasties.

In the first two parts of the novel, Ulrich is drawn into the frantic but essentially vacuous activities set into motion by the Parallel Campaign. Diotima's salon becomes the campaign's unofficial headquarters, and since almost every section of Austrian society wants to influence the direction of the planned jubilee, Musil is able to paint a rich portrait of the epoch's leading character types and their ideas. At Diotima's receptions, Ulrich encounters everyone from members of the imperial government and army General Staff to career diplomats, bourgeois plutocrats, and arriviste poets, and in these chapters Musil comes close to creating a kind of updated, Balzacian human comedy of the Habsburg Empire in its final months. In a separate development, Ulrich also begins to follow the trial of an obsessed sex murderer named "Moosbrugger," who exerts a hold on the Viennese imagination of the day somewhat as Charles Manson did on the American imagination not long ago. Moosbrugger becomes the locus where all the competing discourses of the day pitch their claims for interpretive authority (religious, medical, juridical, philosophical, mystical, etc.), and we hear how each of these discourses fails to incorporate or to convincingly contest the perspective of its rivals. And just as the Parallel Campaign provided Musil with a central focus for the political and economic machinations of Austria's ruling classes, so the Moosbrugger trial turns the novel in a different direction, toward the themes of madness and messianic delusions as these haunt both Ulrich himself and a circle of his private acquaintances, from his frustrated childhood friends Walter and Clarisse to the young right-wing Germanic nationalist Hans Sepp. These minor characters are often deeply compelling in their own right, especially Moosbrugger and Clarisse, whose craziness is disturbingly close to Ulrich's own glimpses of a "second consciousness." Ulrich's thinking strives to break down the binary oppositions that structure the way people make sense out of the world; he is no longer able to believe in the solidity of such antithetical pairings as science versus soul, male versus female, freedom versus necessity, or reason versus imagination. The problem is, though, that a number of other figures in the book not only want to but actually have succeeded in their efforts to break down those oppositions—only these characters are mostly pathological and dangerous. Tracing the separate stories of these characters simultaneously enriches the breadth of the novel's social canvas and, more important, brings into focus the riskiness of Ulrich's decision not to settle for a partial solution to his search for a meaningful new "science of feeling."

But his father's death and his own increasing indifference to the world of power and high politics distance Ulrich more and more from the campaign. In the third, unfinished section of the work ("Into the Millennium"), he gives up his position as the campaign's secretary, temporarily abandons his concern with Moosbrugger, and withdraws almost completely from society in order to pursue his quest for a way to heal the rupture between scientific precision and mystical intensity. His sister, Agathe, whom he rediscovers during the settling of their father's estate, decides to divorce her husband and set up house with Ulrich, and together the two siblings dedicate themselves to learning how "to hold fast to their intimations . . . [of a] second reality . . . a day-bright mysticism . . . [that] mustn't ever be more than an hour old!"[12] The mysticism that Ulrich and Agathe seek is not "a secret through which we enter another world, but only . . . the secret of living in this world differently." Musil never finished his description of Ulrich and Agathe's joint search, but the notes he left behind suggest that this quest, too, ultimately would have failed. In its isolation from the rest of humankind, even as sublime a passion as Ulrich's and Agathe's ends up exhausting itself on the unstable borderline between the ecstatic and the solipsistic.

"Unfortunately, nothing is so hard to achieve as a literary representation of a man thinking."[13] This rueful admission by Musil's narrator crystallizes both the main difficulty as well as the originality of The Man without Qualities. To an extent unprecedented in Western literature, large stretches of the book contain neither a forward-moving action nor inward character development. In their place, we are often given extended sections of pure intellectual-moral speculation, reflections that exist less to illuminate the private passions of a character than to follow the inner logic of a concept with its own independent claims on our attention. This is a kind of novelistic "essayism," a term that exactly translates Musil's loan-word *Essayismus*.

Consider, as a particularly appropriate example of one of the novel's "essays," these passages from a lengthy meditation on the nature of *Essayismus* itself:

> [E]verything he encounters behaves as though it were final and complete. [Yet] he suspects that the given order of things is not as solid as it pretends to be: no thing, no self, no form, no principle, is safe, everything is undergoing an invisible but ceaseless transformation, the unsettled holds more of the future than the settled, and the present is nothing but a hypothesis that has not yet been surmounted . . . later . . . this became an idea no longer connected with the vague word "hypothesis" but with the concept he oddly termed . . . "essay." It was more or less in the way an essay, in the sequence of its paragraphs, explores a thing from many sides without wholly encompassing it—for a thing wholly encompassed suddenly loses its scope and melts down to a concept . . . such an expression is always risky, not yet justified by the prevailing set of affairs, a combination of exact and inexact, of precision and passion. . . . Philosophers are despots who have no armies to command, so they subject the world to their tyranny by locking it up in a system of thought. But . . . there was something in Ulrich's nature that . . . resisted all logical systematizing . . . it was also connected with his chosen term, "essayism" . . . The accepted translation of "essay" as "attempt" contains only vaguely the essential allusion to the literary model, for an essay is not a provisional or incidental expression of a conviction capable of being elevated to a truth . . . or of being exposed as an error . . . An essay is rather the unique and unalterable form assumed by a man's inner life in a decisive thought . . . There have been more than a few such essayists, masters of the inner hovering life [and] . . . their domain lies between religion and knowledge, between example and doctrine, between *amor intellectualis* and poetry. . . . A man who wants the truth becomes a scholar; a man who wants to give free play to his subjectivity may become a writer, but what should a man do who wants something in between?[14]

Essayism is so crucial to Musil because it allows him to express the fullest possible range of human consciousness while avoiding the sterility of premature closure. Since the novel shows us a society caught in a helpless pendulum between sclerosis (Leinsdorf) and cataclysm (Moosbrugger), there is a compelling need for some new, more flexible principle of order. Musil's essayism is no longer a question of genre, it is a way of thinking about and experiencing the world as an unfixable, variegated, and constantly self-transforming phenomenon. Ulrich himself could just as easily be called "the Essayistic Man," and Musil makes clear that the concepts of "essayism" and being "without qualities" are simply twin ways of accounting for the same cast of mind. Even Ulrich's project of taking a year's absence from normal existence in order to explore new ideas and ways of living is itself already a kind of essay. Ulrich's gift as a "master of the hovering life" is to be able to listen to diverse and formally irreconcilable systems of thought without either prejudging them or forcing them into a premature synthesis, and his sharpest irony is reserved for those who insist that only their own explanatory terms are really "true" and "complete." It is only for the insane that everything falls into place, like Moosbrugger, whom Ulrich views as "a rampant metaphor of order."[15] For the truly mad, the whole universe is just a manifestation of their demand for an absolute order based on the impoverished categories of their own egos. Thus, during Moosbrugger's time in jail, Musil gives us a terrifying glimpse of a too-ordered consciousness at its most pathological:

> If Moosbrugger had had a big sword, he'd have drawn it and chopped the head off his chair. He would have chopped the head off the table and the window, the slop bucket, the door. Then he would have set his own head on everything because in this cell there was only one head, his own, and that was as it should be. He could imagine his head sitting on top of things . . . The table was Moosbrugger. The chair was Moosbrugger. The barred window and bolted door were himself.[16]

The chapter from which this quote is taken, called "Moosbrugger Dances," is an uncanny glimpse of the implicit danger in a state of mind that many of the century's most powerful writers had depicted as entirely beneficent. Moosbrugger's delirium is close to a sinister parody of Rilkean inwardness; when the table, chair, window, and door become Moosbrugger, the language has some of the same rhythms and intensities as the epiphanies of "real seeing" in Rilke's *Notebooks of Malte Laurids Brigge*. In his prison cell, Moosbrugger achieves something eerily like the Angel's perspective in the *Duino Elegies* for which Rilke himself spent decades longing. It was crucial for Musil to show the pathological extension of such visionary moments as well as their extraordinary attraction. For a poet like Yeats, the question "How can we tell the dancer from the dance?"[17] is always purely celebratory: the merging of one's inner world with the externally given environment and the perfect interplay of body and spirit are exemplary of a transcendent realization achieved only in rare moments of utter focus like in a dancer's performance or a mystic's trance. In many ways, Musil shared Yeats's and Rilke's conviction that breaking down the difference between self and world is an essential step in attaining the kind of unitary wisdom for which all three writers were seeking. But he is aware, in a way neither Rilke nor Yeats was, that the collapse of boundaries is always also deeply perilous, and that the effects of trying to achieve such a collapse, both for individuals and for societies, have often been catastrophic. Moosbrugger is both inside and outside of normal distinctions. Musil finds a brilliantly unexpected image, one consonant with Moosbrugger's own physically vivid conceptual repertoire, to illustrate the strain required *not* to let one's consciousness expand until it merges violently with everything it encounters:

> It was just that the rubber bands were gone [for Moosbrugger]. Behind every thing or creature, when it tries to get really close to another, is a rubber band, pulling. Otherwise, things might finally go right through one another. Every movement is reined in by a rubber band that won't let a person do quite what he wants. Now, suddenly, all those rubber bands were gone.[18]

It is the hard work of maintaining proportion and balance on which passages like this insist. For all his analysis of the limitations of prosaic reasonableness, Musil is the only one of the five figures treated in this book for whom it was not inherently beneath serious consideration. Indeed, at several points in the novel, Musil suggests that the long-standing Habsburg distaste for extreme measures and radical innovations, combined with its undeniable intellectual and political philistinism, probably contributed as much to the empire's longevity as did any of its more edifying characteristics. The breakdown of that mildly cynical Habsburg accommodationism and its replacement by shrilly competing absolutist ideologies were a far more serious harbinger of crisis than the supposed laxness and decadence with which critics habitually charge the last years of the empire. *The Man without Qualities* makes it clear that far from being too indolent and pleasure-seeking, almost everyone in Vienna is as obsessed with finding his or her own all-transforming new ways of living as are Ulrich, Moosbrugger, and Clarisse. No one, from wealthy industrialists to adulterous housewives, is without a solution to the problems of the age. Ulrich's own skeptical and bemused intelligence needs to be emphasized so strongly in the essayistic passages of parts 1 and 2 in order to balance the reader's awareness that his longing for a mystical "oneness with the world" in which "all affirmations express only a single surging experience"[19] shares an unwelcome family resemblance with Moosbrugger's ecstatic delirium and Clarisse's swirling fantasies.

The similarities between Ulrich and the other characters also ensures that the book is not simply condescending to everyone except its hero. At their best, the essayistic parts of the novel really are essays; that is, they have no absolute authority over any other sections of the book and do not add up to one single, overarching argument. Hence the element of irony in the essays, an irony that is aimed as much at Ulrich's cherished ideas as at the more obviously mockable opinions of the minor characters or of Austrian society in general. This is very different from the essays in novels like Tolstoy's *War and Peace* or Hermann Broch's

The Sleep-Walkers, which are largely without irony about the novel's serious themes and which, consequently, read more like *treatises* than true essays. Tolstoy's and Broch's essays are unmistakable vehicles for ideas that advance the argument of the book as a whole—so much so that they risk making the rest of the narrative seem more like an illustration or instantiation of the judgments reached in the "essays" rather than an independent carrier and revealer of meaning. In one of the late entries in his *Diaries*, Musil tried to define his distinctive kind of irony: "Irony has to contain an element of suffering in it. (Otherwise it is the attitude of a know-it-all.) Enmity and sympathy."[20] In *The Man without Qualities*, even the deranged characters are rarely seen without that crucial "element of suffering." But clarity is ultimately even more important than sympathy, and Musil shows us that figures like Moosbrugger and Clarisse, who mistake their moments of phantasmagoric inward illumination for universal truth, can only react with murderous rage or total dissociation whenever their beliefs are thwarted. On the other hand, our long familiarity with Ulrich's essayism, with its insistence on the *provisional* character of any realization, helps us trust his experiences of transcendent wholeness in part 3, while still, like the narrator himself, keeping a certain critical distance from the full sweep of Ulrich's and Agathe's "second reality." Because Ulrich's scientific and mathematical skepticism coexists with equally powerful yearnings for a condition in which feeling and knowledge would act in concert, neither perspective can ever be sacrificed. Ulrich is no more willing to abandon the rational, analytic categories of pure thought than he can find satisfaction solely within their terms.

Ulrich's essayism may incline toward the merging of exterior and interior perceptions, but it cannot inhabit them exclusively. Unlike Moosbrugger's or Clarisse's delusions, which are always in part compensatory for their thwarted desires and which are regularly redirected by random physical sensations and external stimuli, it is often impossible to specify what prompts a particular chain of thinking in Ulrich. Indeed, it is the *absence* of any readily categorizable motivation for their speculations that distinguishes Ulrich and Agathe from the other figures in the book, whose delight in large, philosophical-sounding pronouncements is wickedly satirized by having the self-serving and self-referential function of their ideas laid bare. The Habsburg aristocrat, Count Leinsdorf, for example, is a marvel of quiet complacency, memorably described as being unable to recognize anything in what he reads, "other than agreement with or mistaken divergence from his own principles"[21] Musil's most vividly realized secondary characters, like the great industrialist and occasional writer of philosophical-cultural tracts Paul Arnheim (modeled after the German tycoon and Weimar foreign minister Walter Rathenau [1867–1922]), all *use* ideas to validate their particular class or professional interests, while society figures like Diotima try on important cultural issues like pieces of prized jewelry designed to confer distinction on whoever wears them. For men with virtually unlimited qualities like Arnheim, the dilemmas that torment Ulrich are only transient, topical disturbances, and Arnheim's self-satisfaction is grounded in the conviction that he already embodies the very synthesis for which Ulrich is futilely searching. When Arnheim loftily declares that what the modern world requires is to unite "capital and culture" (*Besitz und Bildung*), he does so with the comforting knowledge that he possesses both in abundance: "Arnheim's books also had the same kind of self-assurance: the world was in order as soon as Arnheim had given it his consideration."[22]

Each of the secondary characters has fashioned a prison for himself or herself through a false and partial or, more accurately, false *because* partial, worldview. Fundamentally there is something similar between letting one's madness (Moosbrugger and Clarisse) or one's ideology (Leinsdorf and Arnheim) think for one. Moosbrugger, Clarisse, Arnheim, and even the emperor, Franz Joseph himself, want, in their different ways, to be all inclusive—all of them, not just Moosbrugger, are actually "rampant principles of order." Whereas men like Leinsdorf and Arnheim familiarize everything in their world by viewing it as an extension of themselves, Ulrich programmatically defamiliarizes whatever he encounters. While they bring everything back to the expected, to the already known and available formulations, Ulrich tears everything out of its customary frame of reference and makes it part of a deliberately inconclusive new essay. To contest the certainties of the other characters, Ulrich relies on four closely related techniques of resistance. First, he extends what he is given in an unexpected direction. Second, he considers it from a completely different system of thought (e.g., if it is a cultural idea, he will give it a scientific or economic explanation; if it is an economic one, he will analyze it from the perspective of moral theory), thereby creating a cross-analysis of discursive fields in which commonplace assumptions are destabilized as well as defamiliarized. Third, he assigns an inverse moral and psychological value to current ideas in order to test the consequences if what is assumed to be positive is provisionally regarded as negative and vice versa. Fourth, he makes people confront their own stake in whatever system of explanation they cling to, thereby bringing to light its inherently ideological and self-interested function. One odd result of such corrosive scrutiny is that as soon as one of the other characters voices an idea whose attraction we have heard Ulrich himself proclaim, he is immediately driven to challenge it. To Ulrich, these ideas have value only as single elements of an undiscovered new compound; when he suspects that they are being held up as the total solution, they temporarily lose all their appeal.

But the refusal to exploit ideas ideologically, to inflate the limited and fixed perspectives of a class or character into a totalizing explanatory system, greatly raises both the stakes and the potential self-contradiction in the book's quest for *das rechte Leben*, the right life and the right way to live that life. The plot of *The Man without Qualities* is not so much philosophically driven as it is propelled by the search for a philosophy sufficient to motivate a meaningful story. At its core, the novel is continuously about judgment—it is actually about nothing but judgment, about how and what to judge—and yet it ruthlessly and continuously undermines all existing criteria of judgment. How, then, can we judge at all, when what we are looking for are precisely criteria of judgment? The novel keeps reflecting on its own possibility of existing, but since that question is also the point of origin of the whole narrative, there is a sense in which the story not only can't end but cannot even properly begin. When Ulrich says that "we really shouldn't demand action from one another; we should create the conditions that make action possible,"[23] he is not merely speaking of his own quest, but also of Musil's dilemma as a novelist. Several times in the novel, in such passages as "he had always ended up feeling trapped in endless preparations that would never come to fruition,"[24] Ulrich's destiny, Musil's personal anxieties, and the fate of The Man without Qualities itself are clearly linked. Musil increasingly came to feel that it was an impossible task simultaneously to depict actions while exploring the preconditions that would make those actions truly meaningful. The very concept of das rechte Leben implies a hierarchic stability that is counter to the infinite openness and provisional nature of essayism, of remaining "without qualities." If the partiality of Arnheim's and Leinsdorf's ideas is what makes them vulnerable to Musil's irony, why is Ulrich's dedication to finding das rechte Leben any less subject to a critique of its absolutist claims? One of the central problems of Ulrich's quest, and thus of the novel as a whole, is that at its deepest level it wants mutually exclusive things, and in that sense Ulrich's project is dangerously similar to the hopelessness of the Parallelaktion. Paradoxically, though, what rescues the novel from the dangers of its own totalizing ambition is its very "failure" to reach any conclusion. The essayism that fractures its surface and disrupts any movement toward closure is also what gives The Man without Qualities its permanent freshness and sense of intellectual and imaginative daring. The book's density of historical description and social observation are important not merely for the inherent novelistic pleasure they provide, but as the indispensable counterpart to what would otherwise risk becoming a kind of free-floating spiritual autobiography. Ulrich continues to remain socially a man without qualities, not merely a solitary consciousness, both because the world he inhabits is realized with such vivid specificity and because that world keeps generating so many fascinating and preposterous, but historically plausible, characters to set beside him. The book's attention is significantly wider than Ulrich's—hence the discrepancies between the narrator's voice and Ulrich's—and it is able to include a critique of its hero's project as part of its own larger story. The essayistic temperament can never permanently privilege any single perspective, not even one "without qualities," and while the novel as a whole takes Ulrich's longing for das rechte Leben almost as seriously as he himself does, in the end, that search remains only the most important of the multiple, mutually antagonistic quests whose unfolding constitutes the book's real story.

* * *

Musil saw his Vienna as both uniquely itself and as "nothing but a particularly clear-cut case of the modern world."[25] But readers of *The Man without Qualities* know from the outset that the particular world the novel describes has very little time left before perishing in the conflagration of World War I. Yet Musil does not use the reader's knowledge of the empire's imminent dissolution as the basis for representing the actions and hopes of the characters in the book as absurd, nor is his ironic perspective on contemporary political events based on their eventual outcome.[26] The Parallel Campaign, for example, is not ludicrous *because* the emperor it planned to honor would be dead and his dynasty overthrown before the celebration's announced date. On the contrary, in its intellectual incoherence and ideological blindness, the campaign was already thoroughly ludicrous from the moment of its conception. In the salons and ministries of Vienna in the years before the war, the chance of a general European conflict is kept constantly in mind, but it is presented as only one of a wide range of possibilities, and avoiding such an outcome is, in fact, the chief purpose of many of the characters in Musil's book. Most of what takes place politically is a result of the law of unintended consequences, and nothing better illustrates this than the fact that the nebulous Parallel Campaign, originally conceived as an anti-Prussian maneuver, will soon give way to the all-too-real parallel action of the Austrian and German armies marching as allies to their joint destruction. *The Man without Qualities* is full of intimations of the coming war, but it is just as resonant with suggestions that such a cataclysm can be prevented. The important point is that Musil skillfully allows the whole range of ideas and hopes held by his characters *in 1913* to be heard clearly on their own terms. He regularly satirizes all of his characters' positions, but only when their blindness and self-deception are already fully demonstrable in the context of their own day, not when they fail to foresee the future accurately.

The Man without Qualities shows us that there is no inevitable trajectory to events: the Parallel Campaign stumbles toward the war quite against the intentions of most of its members. There is no overarching, secret authority or force planning everything and moving history along a predetermined path. Competing centers of power (foreign affairs [Tuzzi], the army [Stumm von Bordwehr], and international finance [Arnheim]) have separate and often competing agendas. They form temporary and rapidly changing alliances, often with groups whose purpose and raison d'être are actually antithetical to their own. At a certain point, it sometimes happens that the particular "local" alliances that have coalesced for that moment alone find themselves bound together for good into a single long-term aim by the pressures of a larger event that none of them had expected, like the outbreak of a continent-engulfing war. But it is important to recall that the alliances' individual members did not seek the war as their principal objective, nor did they envisage any permanent link to one another. For example, Austria's foreign service and army tried repeatedly to forge alliances that would prevent the Habsburg Empire from becoming Prussia's junior partner. Yet that is precisely what it did become, against all the aspirations of its most skilled leaders. In the course of the novel, we see how the fumblings of the Parallel Campaign helped cement a German-Austrian alliance, which was the one goal undesired by anyone involved in its initial conception.

Musil's novelistic solution to the epistemological problems raised by the narration of historical events whose outcome is already known is exemplary in its fairness. Since it is impossible for the reader to suspend a knowledge of the book's historical aftermath, the narrator deliberately plays on that knowledge, not to exploit it for the emotional intensities it might add to the story, but rather to undermine any sense of historical inevitability. The dense network of contradictory voices and ideas represented in the book makes the reader's faith in a superior, because subsequent, vantage point impossible. There are so many plausible scenarios for the future sketched out in *The Man without Qualities*, so many different hopes and expectations expressed by characters in a position to make astute forecasts, that the novel swarms with projections of mutually exclusive prospects. Inevitably, though, because we know which of these projected futures came to pass, we are tempted to pay special attention whenever any character seems to articulate as the likeliest possibility what actually happened in 1914. Musil is especially inventive at finding effective ways to subvert this impulse, to make clear, that is, the absurdity of judging his book's characters by the accuracy of their historical prognoses. For example, perhaps the most benevolently accommodating character in the entire novel is Ulrich's friend General Stumm von Bordwehr, who is sent by the General Staff to represent the army at Diotima's salon. Instead of the conventional postwar literary representation of senior officers as callous monsters, completely without any regard for human life, Musil goes out of his way to show Stumm as both kindhearted and utterly unbelligerent, all the while knowing that the novel's readers can never entirely forget that it is precisely men like Stumm who will shortly be leading the Imperial Army into mass slaughter. Musil then complicates this already subtle play between the novel's and the reader's different temporal horizons by having the usually ridiculous Diotima be more prescient than Ulrich when it comes to foreseeing the likelihood of a general war. It is Diotima who is right about what Stumm will end up doing. She says of him, "he makes me think of death," and when Ulrich lightheartedly replies, "an uncommonly life-loving figure of Death," Diotima's insistence that Stumm fills her "with an indescribable, incomprehensible, dreamlike fear" is decidedly more prophetic.[27] If either Ulrich or the narrator were to predict the coming war, their foreshadowing would risk endowing that outcome with the aura of historical inevitability. But since it is the usually self-deluded Diotima who guesses correctly, the war becomes just one of the possibilities in the air at the time. Musil repeatedly makes fun of the urge to endow a specific moment with greater portentousness strictly because of what actually ensued: "Time was making a fresh start then (it does so all the time). . . .

there was great excitement everywhere around the turn of 1913–1914. But two years or five years earlier there had also been much excitement."[28]

The war is never seen as "inevitable" by Musil, for the very good reason that nothing in history can be so considered. The war is indisputably a pivotal turning point in world history, but its historical magnitude gives it no retrospective authority over the events narrated in *The Man without Qualities*. History is not destiny. The most satiric parts of Musil's novel describe a world in stasis or in a self-perpetuating muddle, rather than on the verge of disintegration. The Habsburg Empire that we actually are shown could just as easily have lasted for many years more, just as, for example, the Ottoman Empire survived for more than a century after observers were certain of its imminent dissolution. The disintegration certainly happened, but occurrence, as *The Man without Qualities* regularly instructs us, does not imply necessity.

Yet just as Ulrich is deeply frustrated by the gulf separating modern man's expert knowledge in the professional and scientific areas of life from the uncritical assumptions with which he interprets the world in his private psychological and moral life, so the novel as a whole seeks to undo the narrative conventions by which the reader imposes a linear, scripted pattern on the motility of historical events and individual psyches. Musil's irony works so effectively because he expects readers to approach a novel set on the eve of the Great War as though it would manifest all the familiar devices of deterministic inevitability. Thus we, too, are already "set up" by our own expectations to undergo the shock of realizing that everyone, not just the book's characters, indulges in no-longer-credible patterns of thinking. What is satirized in Musil's descriptions is not the psychological makeup of the characters, but their habits of thought, and since those same habits still largely govern how we make sense of our world, we are denied the position of superiority usually occupied by readers of satires. Musil's typically ironic/serious way of insisting on the speciousness of fixed interpretive categories is to deny the attribute of inevitability even to divine creation: "God Himself probably preferred to speak of His world in the subjunctive of possibility . . . for God creates the world and thinks while He is at it that it could just as well be done differently."[29] And this aphorism exactly parallels the dilemma at the heart of the new kind of novel Musil was striving to create.

Musil undertook the perhaps irreconcilable duties of creating a fully plausible, densely realized world while still indicating that "it could just as well be done differently." And so, irrespective of some posthumous drafts in which Musil briefly tries out having Ulrich go into combat, it is unlikely that the war could have been inserted successfully into the novel. Only by setting his narrative before the outbreak of hostilities can Musil guarantee that neither his characters nor his narrator speaks with predictive historical certainty. Since Musil is so concerned to show that many things can be imagined as likely to happen, and that history is not driven by any rational principle or internal logic that would let the future be accurately predicted, he is also particularly careful not to allow the war to undermine the novel's fidelity to a sense of multifarious possibilities (*Möglichkeitssinn*). To include the war directly would risk giving it the privilege of being not just an *event* in the narrative, but rather its *meaning*, and this, precisely, is what Musil regarded as unacceptable. But simply at the level of composing a coherent work of art, Musil's refusal to use the war as an externally validated closure to his book left him with an impossible struggle to create a structure that would provide a narratable resolution to his theoretical and ethical requirements. That he failed to do so is clear not only from the incompleteness of the novel at the time of his death, but also from the nature of the last sections he actually published and the enormous mass of drafts and fragments he left behind. A variety of reasons—including depression over the lack of an audience, an intermittent but long-standing "writer's block," intellectual exhaustion, and the financial uncertainties of an exile's life—have all been advanced to explain Musil's inability to complete his book. But once Musil rejected ending the novel with the melodramatic thunderclap of the outbreak of war (say, for example, with the reading of a telegram announcing Franz Ferdinand's assassination at what would then obviously become the last meeting of the Parallel Campaign), the novel had to remain unfinished for strictly internal reasons.

The *Man without Qualities* is a work that, for all its biting irony, struggles to achieve not a distance from the world, but an adequacy to the world's inherent complexity. The problem, in its simplest terms, is that the exclusion of the war turns the various contradictory futures projected by the book's different characters into permanently available possibilities. That, in turn, makes the novel itself permanently unresolvable into an outcome of any kind, since the choice of an ending counter to the real, historical one would have the intolerable effect of relegating the entirety of *The Man without Qualities* to the realm of the fantastical. Musil was trapped between closure and counterhistory: closure would mean ending the story with the war, counterhistory would mean allowing the empire to continue indefinitely, and neither solution was acceptable. In *The Enthusiasts*, one of the characters cries out, "But then life always makes you choose between two possibilities, and you always feel: One is missing! Always one—the uninvented third possibility."[30] But Musil, to his dismay, found that his novel, too, was making him choose between two equally inadequate possibilities. Inventing a third one was the hopeless goal that he had set himself in order to end the novel on his own terms, and he preferred leaving everything in fragments rather than imposing an artificial solution in which he could not believe. The tension between closure and counterhistory is actually symmetrical with that of wanting both the stability of *das rechte Leben* and the permanent fluidity of essayism. It is equally impossible to narrate the war or to trace the lineaments of a utopian way of life entirely "in the subjunctive case." Moreover, a resolution in the text that remained entirely private but had no correspondence in or influence upon the public world would have been unsatisfactory and, by Musil's standards, unprincipled. That is no doubt why he deliberately rejected what would have been the readily narratable, but purely aesthetic solution of having Ulrich decide to write about his failed attempt to find *das rechte Leben* in a book that we retroactively understand is the very novel we have just finished reading. Such a sub-Proustian strategy had no appeal for Musil, in part because he was unconvinced about the redemptive power of art and in part because doing so would risk collapsing the indispensable difference between Ulrich and the narrator. But precisely the same reasons make even the illuminations of what Ulrich and Agathe call their "holy conversations" on the nature of love impossible to use as a conclusion. Tempted though he clearly was to abandon the novel's public and historical issues for the inwardness of Ulrich's and Agathe's union, Musil ultimately decided, on what I think were primarily ethical grounds, to make clear that even these two marvelously prepared lovers ultimately fail to sustain the "incomparable birth of the spirit out of darkness."[31] If too much were claimed for it, Agathe's and Ulrich's love would end up providing an emotional-erotic "answer" to his quest in precisely the same way that a successful "slogan" would solve the Parallel Campaign's search for a unifying national theme, and hence it would be just as vulnerable to essayistic mockery.

And yet, because they are not made to serve as the climactic revelations on which the novel ends, the posthumous fragments about Ulrich's and Agathe's relationship are able to contain some of the book's most moving passages. The satiric tone of the earlier portions drops away. Musil's spiritual yearning begins to penetrate Ulrich's and Agathe's discussions, and so does his extensive reading in the Church Fathers and Christian mystics. Finally their "understanding gives way to irrepressible astonishment."[32] Their love story encompasses intellect, sexual passion, transcendence, and rootedness in the world in a way that, with the sole exception of Rilke's late poetry, is unique in postmedieval literature. Many of their dialogues are set in the garden of the house they now share, and in Ulrich's astonishment at his unexpected happiness, Musil undoubtedly intended us to hear an echo of the Song of Solomon's wonderful phrase, "A garden inclosed is my sister, my spouse" (Song of Sol. 4:12, King James Bible). The intense inwardness of some of Ulrich's and Agathe's meditations come close to finding a prose equivalent for the interpenetration between subject and object, self and world, that the *Duino Elegies* celebrate. Sometimes, in reading these chapters, it is as if we are encountering a consciousness simultaneously imbued with the ecstatic longing of a great mystic and the fastidious rationality of a master logician:

Not only do external relationships melt away and re-form in the whispering enclosures of light and shadow, but the inner relationships, too, move closer together in a new way . . . And it is not the mouth that pours out its adoration but the body, which, from head to foot, is stretched taut in exaltation above the darkness of the earth and beneath the light of the heavens, oscillating between two stars. And the whispering with one's companion is full of a quite unknown sensuality, which is not the sensuality of an individual human being but of all that is earthly, of all that penetrates perception and sensation, the suddenly revealed tenderness of the world that incessantly touches all our senses and is touched by them.[33]

For the first time in the book, there are extended dialogues in which it is not always Ulrich's voice that is endowed with expository authority. Agathe often helps Ulrich understand his own experiences by giving him a series of images that come closer to what he is feeling and thinking than any of his own attempts at a more comprehensive formulation:

I suggest you try looking at a mirror in the night: it's dark, it's black, you see almost nothing at all; and yet this nothing is something quite distinctly different from the nothing of the rest of the darkness. You sense the glass, the doubling of depth, some kind of remnant of the ability to shimmer—and yet you perceive nothing at all![34]

How do you bring closure to what is, by definition, provisional? At their best, these fragmentary chapters are working toward a new mode of writing that might be called ecstatic essayism, so deliberately do they take up and rework in a heightened key some of the fundamental motifs of earlier sections. The startling shifts in Musil's tone, from analytic to imagistic, and from aloofly ironical to soaringly impassioned, come very close to fashioning a convincing linguistic correlative for the union of lucidity and self-transcendence that Ulrich and Agathe set out to find. But Musil's language also shows the gradual winding down of that transcendence, its erosion by the forces of exhaustion and enervation. A private revelation, even one as intense and as seemingly earned as Ulrich's and Agathe's, is shown to be as vulnerable to the laws of entropy as the society the lovers had sought to leave behind. Nowhere is Musil's integrity more visible than in his refusal to make these two figures, in whom he himself had clearly invested so many of his own hopes as well as the whole destiny of his novel, emerge as convincing alternatives to the quotidian, historical reality of the other characters. Musil's novel lets us glimpse the flicker of a possible, redemptive integrity, but at the end, it returns us to the moment before the catastrophe with which the whole book began. In a way, nothing has happened in the course of this immense, incomplete, and uncompletable novel. But like Agathe's mirror, we are profoundly different for having looked at that nothing with receptive eyes. In its deliberate failure to cohere into a definable plot, *The Man without Qualities* explicitly reveals itself, in a way few novels of comparable ambition do, to be written not only *about* history, but from *within* it as well.

Earlier, I quoted Musil's injunction to himself never to permit his sense of irony to serve as merely the facile demonstration of an isolate superiority. Musilian irony must always "contain an element of suffering in it,"[35] precisely because irony and suffering are the direct emotional and stylistic correlates of Musil's demand for precision and soul. The whole of *The Man without Qualities* shows how simultaneously potent and fragile that amalgam can be. Musil placed extraordinary, indeed impossible, demands on himself as a writer and thinker, but he understood better than almost anyone else how much still remained to be done before we can achieve a way to talk about what matters most to us without relying on outworn premises and discredited conventions. For Musil, everything, including the shape and rhythm of our own sentences, should have the freshness of a new discovery. His definition of good writing in the *Diaries* has a generosity of responsiveness to the specific moment that is almost profligate in its refusal to keep anything back: "Something is well-written if, after some time, it strikes one as alien—one would be incapable of writing it that way a second time. Such an idea (expression) did not come from the fund that is available for daily expenditure."[36] To read Musil is to encounter both the risks and the sheer excitement of that kind of writing.

3

Martin Heidegger
Judgment Terminal and Interminable

Does it really matter, in the end, what sort of man or woman produced the works that compel our attention? Historically, the issue has been framed in many different rhetorics. In *Rameau's Nephew*, the most prescient and unsettling of the eighteenth century's speculative fictions, Denis Diderot dramatized the long-standing debate about the ethical responsibility of a genius in the following exchange:

> HE: Men of genius are only good for one thing, and apart from that, nothing. They don't know what it means to be citizens, fathers, mothers, brothers, relations, friends . . .
> I: Which would you prefer: that Racine had been a worthy person . . . giving his wife a legitimate baby once a year, a good husband, good father, good uncle, good neighbor, an honest tradesman, but nothing more; or that he had been a rogue, a traitor, ambitious, envious, spiteful, but the creator of *Andromaque, Brittanicus, Iphigénie, Phèdre, Athalie?*[1]

Today, the disjunction between imaginative intelligence and character is a cultural commonplace, and yet we have never entirely stopped asking whether there is a point at which a basic shabbiness of soul must disfigure any works that such a person produces. A century and a half after Diderot, with his ethical understanding decisively sharpened by the Dreyfus case, Marcel Proust recast the whole question in terms whose pertinence has become increasingly evident with each new decade. So tolerant of the sexual, financial, and careerist derelictions of his characters, Proust insisted on a categorical difference between offenses committed for private ends and offenses perpetrated on behalf of a political evil, declaring that "we forgive the crimes of individuals, but not their participation in a collective crime."[2]

All of the significant arguments invoked in "the case of Martin Heidegger"— the unpalatable but indisputable fact that one of the twentieth century's most

influential and original philosophers was, for a while at least, a convinced Nazi—
recapitulate either the open-minded puzzlement of Diderot's conversationalists or
the finality of Proust's austere verdict. And yet, our familiarity with the various
positions that have been taken about Heidegger's politics, the ease with which we
can usually deduce the main contours of successive new accounts from a few initial
sentences, far from exhausting the controversy seem only to provoke ever more
voices to enter the debate. Indeed, so heated and prolonged a controversy about
the degree of connection between the philosophy, the politics, and the personal
character of a reclusive man, most of whose life was spent as a university professor,
who occupied no nationally important political office, and who scarcely ever left his
native province, let alone his country, is more surprising than any of the specific
interpretations of that relationship. Not only is the bibliography of secondary
studies devoted to Heidegger already by far the largest of any twentieth-century
philosopher, but the disproportion is actually increasing. The contentiousness
of the debate about Heidegger and the participation in it of important figures
from almost every continent and perspective is unprecedented, and to dismiss the
phenomenon as mere journalistic chatter is itself just a manifestation of intellectual
carelessness. The real philistinism, it seems to me, is to be found in the view
that there is nothing really important at stake, that nothing Heidegger did or
wrote apart from his strictly philosophical publications should have any bearing
on how we respond to those ideas and those texts, and that his own allegiances and
commitments are no more than ephemeral side issues about which it is pointless to
speculate since they are irrelevant to any serious consideration of his significance
as a thinker.

To the extent that we are willing to take Heidegger seriously at all, we
cannot repudiate questions about his moral and political choices by arguing that
we are largely unconcerned about the personal virtue or political affiliations of
philosophers from earlier centuries, and so we ought to approach Heidegger
with the same diffidence. Admittedly, episodes like Plato's ill-fated involvement
with Dionysius II of Syracuse or Hegel's delight in being decorated by Frederick
William III of Prussia play little role in our evaluation of either philosopher's
work. But our relationship to Heidegger is different, and this is so for reasons
his own thinking best explains. Even though lifelong admirers like Hannah Arendt
explicitly compared Heidegger's involvement with National Socialism to Plato's
two visits to the tyrant of Syracuse, it is fundamental to Heidegger's teaching that
we are creatures of time who exist in a specific historical moment, not in some
abstract, atemporal realm, and it is from within our own temporal horizon that our
primary judgments are always made. Our knowledge of the Nazi death camps is a
crucial element of the world into which we ourselves have been "thrown," to use
Heidegger's charged term, and it is senseless to expect that we should somehow
bracket the pressures and claims of that grim temporal knowledge when we reflect

on Heidegger's own writings. I suppose that one may imagine a future when Nazism is as distant a historical memory as the Syracusan politics of Plato's day, and then, perhaps, the relationship between Heidegger's political commitments and his philosophy will be of interest only to the specialists in such questions. But we are not living in that future yet.

Moreover, although it is routinely insisted upon by his advocates, the whole distinction between the canonical texts that supposedly constitute Heidegger's authentic reflections and a secondary body of ephemeral writings that are merely "private" expressions and hence have no bearing on his real work as a thinker remains highly problematic. At the very least, such a dichotomy contradicts one of the cardinal principles of his own project. No philosopher has done more than Heidegger to undermine the stability of precisely these kinds of conventional categories. One of his enduring legacies is to have greatly extended our awareness of what can ground a philosophical discourse. Many of his own most searching meditations are careful teasings-out of the theoretical richness of such philosophically unexpected subjects as a single fragment of Anaximander, a painting by Van Gogh, or a few lyrics by Hölderlin or Rilke. In light of such a practice, it is hard to justify deciding ahead of time, and merely on the basis of genre or occasion, which of Heidegger's own words should count as his legitimate philosophical legacy and which can be ignored as inconsequential. It is even more dubious to rely on such distinctions to settle the problem of the moral accountability of his thinking.

In fact, Heidegger is remarkable for the persistence with which he clung to his belief in the fundamental validity of his political and cultural insights, and for his insistence on grounding those perceptions in his larger philosophical project. Nothing in his writings suggests that Heidegger sought to distinguish between his texts according to whether they treated contemporary historical and political conditions or more strictly traditional philosophical problems, nor did he classify them according to their initial occasion and audience. It is true that Heidegger entirely disavowed or reinterpreted away politically compromising documents from the Nazi era when these jeopardized his postwar career, notably his Rector's Address on "The Self-Assertion of the German University" delivered at the University of Freiburg on May 27, 1933, and published shortly thereafter,[3] and his "Appeal to German Students" of a few months later, which included the exhortation: "Let not axioms or 'ideas' be the rules of your Being. The Führer himself and alone is the present and future German reality and its law."[4] Immediately upon reading the Rector's Address, Benedetto Croce described it as "stupid and servile at the same time,"[5] and in subsequent years, Heidegger tried to distance himself from it as much as possible. But there were equally problematic statements that were never completely erased, and the texts in which these assertions appear must figure in any listing, no matter how tendentiously selected, of Heidegger's principal writings.

Thus, in 1953, when he published *An Introduction to Metaphysics*, based on lectures he first delivered in 1935, Heidegger made a point of retaining a sentence about "the inner truth and greatness of this movement," referring to National Socialism. He even specified wherein that inner truth and greatness lay: "namely, the encounter between planetary technology and modern man."[6] Since that "encounter" is perhaps the most powerful and abiding of all Heidegger's postwar concerns, to link its theorization to an unrealized potential within Nazism, and to do so eight years after the collapse of Hitler's Reich, shows a greater steadfastness in Heidegger's political vision than his apologists are comfortable admitting.

Similarly, in the Bremen lectures of 1949, which became the basis for his major essay on "The Question Concerning Technology,"[7] Heidegger makes clear that in his view the extermination of European Jewry was merely one more instantiation of the abuse of technology—lamentable, no doubt, but no more important or grievous than the mechanization of agriculture. All of technology's destructive effects are treated as equivalent manifestations of a deeper crisis, and the refusal to distinguish hierarchically between these effects is entirely deliberate and polemical, part of a theoretical claim about modernity that Heidegger never ceased reiterating:

> Agriculture is now a mechanized food industry, in essence the same as the manufacture of corpses in the gas chambers and extermination camps, the same as the blockade and starvation of the countryside, the same as the production of the hydrogen bombs.[8]

This programmatic leveling of differences is characteristic of his pronouncements on cultural-political questions throughout his writing. It occurs in his best-known works as regularly as in his occasional pieces, and it is as much a part of his philosophical legacy as the analysis of human temporality and care (*Sorge*) in *Being and Time*. Jürgen Habermas usefully labeled this tendency "abstraction via essentialization,"[9] and it is worth remarking how little is required by way of argumentation to perform this "essentialization." Especially striking is how the strategic use of the phrase "in essence the same as" does all the work of uniting diverse events into a single manifold without ever specifying what common features confirm the fundamental equivalence of all the elements on his list.

It was precisely this technique that enabled Heidegger to declare in 1935 that America and Stalinist Russia are "metaphysically speaking, the same."[10] Heidegger regularly asserts the existence of a deeper stratum of truth or reality that determines all the various manifestations of the surface, and it is from the perspective of that primal, grounding reality that the epiphenomena we naively regard as incommensurate can be seen as interchangeable. It is also from this foundational, all-determining first reality that Heidegger's speech implicitly claims to issue, and the story that it wants to tell is nothing less than the historical fate of Being itself.

It is a discourse whose sweep can either thrill or repel, depending in part on the listener's receptivity to the glamour of metaphysical melodrama, but it is not one that can plausibly be differentiated into such secondary and conventionally discrete categories as politics, aesthetics, and philosophy.

If we now return to *Rameau's Nephew*, we can see that in one vital regard the case debated by the interlocutors in Diderot's dialogue is significantly simpler than the questions raised by Heidegger's life and work. Diderot speculates about a genius who was also a thoroughly wicked man, but there is no suggestion of any direct imaginative entailment linking the immortal works to the immorality of the artist who produced them. The ambition, the envy, and the spite attributed to Racine's personality are not interpreted, as they very plausibly might have been, as being imprinted anywhere in his plays, let alone as having been crucial to the creation of Racine's psychologically tortured and self-divided characters. The man and the work are regarded, rather, as mutually independent, and the quarrel turns on how much we should let our knowledge of the artist's personal failings affect our pleasure in his works. In this sense, many recent defenses of Heidegger do little more than offer more modern-sounding versions of Diderot's argument. For example, Richard Rorty wants us to judge Heidegger's philosophical work entirely apart from his politics because "being an original philosopher is like being an original mathematician . . . it is the result of some neural kink that occurs independently of other kinks."[11] But the whole pertinence of such a sharp demarcation is itself one of the chief areas of contention in the debate about Heidegger. As Habermas points out, "what is at issue here is not the relation between the *life* and the work of Heidegger, since that formulation begs the crucial question whether Heidegger's political views should be considered part of his work."[12]

One way to bring Habermas's point into sharper focus is to consider how different the stakes are when such questions are raised about the political behavior of a gifted conductor such as Herbert von Karajan or a singer of unequaled musical intelligence such as Elisabeth Schwarzkopf. Immediately after the war, both artists were accused of complicity with Nazism and both refuted the charge by claiming a fundamental indifference to and naïveté about politics. I am not concerned here to intervene in the controversies about either musician's life. I want only to point out that it has proven much easier to separate artistic accomplishments like von Karajan's or Schwarzkopf's from their politics than to draw the same lines in the case of a philosopher. Someone might choose, for a multitude of understandable reasons, not to purchase a recording by a musician suspected of having been a Nazi, but it would be much harder to establish the more general case that their performances necessarily manifest their political sympathies. But when Heidegger describes his thinking as a "dialogue with the world's destiny,"[13] and offers a diagnosis of our perilous historical situation predicated on his "grasping the basic features of the universal technological age now beginning,"[14] then the question of whether or not his political views are an inextricable part of his philosophical teaching is unavoidable. As the German philosopher Otto Pöggeler puts it, "whoever [wants] . . . to appropriate initiatives and to learn from him must realize that in the 1930's, Heidegger himself placed the decision about the truth of Being as he sought it in a political context."[15] But beyond any questions specific to Heidegger, the functions of philosophical discourse in our culture—the expectations we have of it, the ways we make sense of it, and the themes it both addresses and creates—differ essentially from those of mathematics or music, and so, too, do the questions we can legitimately ask about its political and moral foundation. Rorty's specialized and strictly professional definition of philosophy, one which separates entirely the life from the ideas, is thoroughly complicit with the kind of technological, divisive, and fragmented way of thinking and living that Heidegger specifically criticizes. To defend Heidegger by advancing a series of claims that the core of his thinking is intended to contest is bound to seem strained. To Heidegger, thinking is not merely one academic discipline among many—it is "the basic occurrence of *Dasein*"[16] and as such is inseparable from the fundamental question of how to live. Another powerful countermodel to the strictly technical and academic view of philosophy has been offered recently by Alexander Nehamas, who takes up the Socratic tradition of regarding philosophy as the discovery and fashioning of an "art of living." Nehamas links philosophy's loss of cultural authority—something which Heidegger, too, although from an entirely different perspective and tradition, also laments—to the abdication of the classical notion that a person's life should be in harmony with the philosophy he or she espouses:

> Philosophy [today] also has few implications for the life of those who practice it. What philosophers study makes no more claim to affecting their personal lives than the work of physicists, mathematicians, or economists is expected to affect theirs. And yet there is a lingering sense in most people as well as in a few philosophers that somehow this is not how matters should be, a sense of puzzlement and even of disappointment that the lives of philosophers do not reflect their convictions.[17]

Yet to acknowledge the legitimacy of the question about the relationship between Heidegger's thinking and his life should not imply that one has already decided how it must be answered. In practice, though, the movement from raising the issue to resolving it has tended to be disconcertingly swift. There have been a number of scrupulous studies in English, some entirely critical, others selectively exculpatory, about the relationship between Heidegger's politics and the rest of his philosophical work, especially Richard Wolin's *Politics of Being: The Political Thought of*

Martin Heidegger (1990), Tom Rockmore's *On Heidegger's Nazism and Philosophy* (1992), Leslie Paul Thiele's *Timely Meditations: Martin Heidegger and Postmodern Politics* (1995), Berel Lang's *Heidegger's Silence* (1996), Julian Young's *Heidegger, Philosophy, Nazism* (1997), and Johannes Fritsche's *Historical Destiny and National Socialism in Heidegger's "Being and Time"* (1999). But many otherwise intellectually discriminating figures have shown little hesitation in responding as though the case were self-evident. Early in 1960, for example, Gilbert Ryle, who had favorably reviewed *Being and Time* when it first appeared, supposedly concluded that Heidegger's deficiencies of character are sufficient to make his philosophical writing necessarily second rate. Ryle's verdict as it has come down to us seems straightforward enough: "Bad man. Can't be a good philosopher."[18] Hans-Georg Gadamer settles the question with equal ease, although from the opposite side: to Gadamer, the solution is "simple" as soon as one recognizes that Heidegger was "the greatest of thinkers, but the smallest of men."[19] For neither Ryle nor Gadamer does answering the question about the relationship between Heidegger's life and Heidegger's philosophy require any strenuous reflection or extended argumentation. Neither Ryle's laconic dryness nor Gadamer's cozy "simplicity" engages the issues in a satisfying way. Even less persuasive are debates conducted largely in hand-me-down versions of Heidegger's own idiolect, as though his vocabulary and syntax could be directly imported into comments on him without flooding the discourse. Especially in France, and in certain circles in the American academy, the controversy about Heidegger has also been merged, to no one's advantage, with the logically and historically separate issue of the ethical status of deconstruction. Reading these debates almost makes comprehensible Heidegger's odd boast that "when they [the French] begin to think, they speak German. They assure me they could not manage with their language."[20] No doubt Jean-François Lyotard had this kind of intellectual-linguistic genealogy in mind when, with only superficial irony, he described the "scandal" that arose after the publication, in 1987, of Victor Farías's *Heidegger and Nazism* as "a French affair" ("L'affaire Heidegger est une affaire 'française'").[21] But whatever the extent of deconstruction's indebtedness to and difference from Heidegger, and no matter how simultaneously preening and prickly most of the responses by Derrida and his followers to the Heidegger controversy are, a proper assessment of Derridean philosophy cannot depend directly on what sense we make of the relationship between Heidegger's political and his philosophical work.

Even if we suspend any consideration of Heidegger's often shabby personal behavior and limit the inquiry strictly to the relationship between his publicly expressed political views and his philosophy, it is rare to find any intellectually significant dialogue between his defenders and his critics. For Adorno, Heidegger's thinking is unmistakably "fascist right down to its innermost components."[22] Rorty is equally convinced that "Heidegger was only accidentally a Nazi."[23] Both descriptions strike me as trivial. It is no clearer how Adorno's description might apply to the entirety of Heidegger's writings than it is how someone who took himself, his ideas, and his public persona as seriously as Heidegger did could have been only an "accidental" Nazi. If Adorno is right, then by now Heidegger's thinking would likely have fallen into the same oblivion as the works of such philosophical champions of National Socialism as Alfred Bäumler, Ernst Krieck, Erich Jaensch, or Arnold Gehlen. They, at any rate, had no doubt about the differences between Heidegger's philosophy and their own. Jaensch, it is worth noting, described Heidegger in the following terms to senior Nazi officials in charge of education:

> Heidegger's thought is characterized by the same obsession with hairsplitting distinctions as Talmudic thought. That is why it holds such an extraordinary fascination for Jews, persons of Jewish ancestry and others with a similar mental make-up.[24]

Yet to adopt Rorty's line, and to conclude that there is only a fortuitous connection between Heidegger's philosophy and his pronouncements championing National Socialism, risks trivializing the entirety of his project. Such a position has, as its unacknowledged presupposition, precisely the narrow, professional understanding of philosophical thinking that it was perhaps Heidegger's greatest single ambition to overthrow. There are defenses of a thinker that are just as perilous as any all-encompassing condemnation.

Heidegger's preface to his lectures on Aristotle limited the biographical information he considered worth noting to this sparse sequence: "he was born, worked, and died."[25] Elsewhere, though, he insisted that "everything great arises from man's rootedness in his homeland and tradition,"[26] and he repeatedly emphasized the shaping influence of his native region on his thinking. Like his favorite poets and dramatists, Heidegger placed tremendous emphasis on the revelatory potential of the local, and he felt only contempt for anything that bore traces of cosmopolitanism: "Does not the flourishing of any genuine work depend upon its roots in a native soil?"[27] Owing in part to considerations like these, he declined invitations, in 1930 and 1933, to leave Freiburg for a more prestigious professorship in Berlin.

Heidegger was born in Messkirch in 1889 and died there in 1976. The town was only a short distance from Freiburg, where Heidegger first enrolled as a Catholic theology student in 1909. Even when he discontinued his clerical training and turned to logic, natural sciences, and phenomenology, Heidegger only changed supervisors, not universities. Indeed, with the exception of five years at Marburg between 1923 and 1928, almost the entirety of Heidegger's adult life was spent in Freiburg, first as a student, then as Edmund Husserl's assistant from 1918 to 1923, and finally, beginning in 1928, as Husserl's successor. A detailed chronology of Heidegger's life would read largely like a catalog of publications and talks, with a notable meagerness of dramatic incidents. The one decisive exception to a life of routine academic ambitions and rhythms stands out precisely for being so uncharacteristic—Heidegger's openly pro-Nazi activities, which began when he joined the party on May 1, 1933; dominated his brief, unsuccessful tenure as rector of the university from May 1933 to April 1934; and were still clearly in evidence as late as his lecture visit to Rome in 1936, when he wore his party badge everywhere. Heidegger grew "disillusioned" with Nazism only when it became obvious that the party had no intention of making him its philosophical mentor. On the contrary, the Nazi hierarchy regarded him with some suspicion for having developed "his own private National Socialism" (*Privat-Nationalsozialismus*),[28] which differed in significant ways from the official version. But it seems that the chief intellectual difference he had with the government was that he considered the Nazis insufficiently true to their founding principles: they were, he thought, not radical and resolute enough. Thus, in 1943, Heidegger wrote: "The planet is in flames. The essence of man is out of joint. Only from the Germans can there come a world-historical reflection—if, that is, they find and preserve their 'Germanness' [*das Deutsche*]."[29] The notion that "Germanness" might need to be "preserved" is at least comprehensible as a kind of patriotic rallying cry in the context of a clearly impending military defeat; however, the idea that "das Deutsche" actually might still need to be "found" is startling, since that is precisely what Hitler always claimed as one of his own central accomplishments. But even after his "inner reservations" made Heidegger stop speaking out openly on contemporary political issues, he continued to pay his party membership dues until the end of the war. Indeed, in this sphere, as in every other, Heidegger was extraordinarily circumspect, voicing whatever ideological or theoretical reservations he might have had about the Reich's political direction through the Aesopian form of a series of lectures on Nietzsche's "will to power." There is remarkably little sign in Heidegger's personal life of the "resolve" that his thinking endows with so much prestige. A kind of prudential caution marks his whole existence, and nothing, not even the passionate love affair that he began in 1924 with his then eighteen-year-old student, Hannah Arendt, was allowed to imperil his academic career or undermine the domestic tranquillity that his wife, Elfriede, took care to provide for him.

It is impossible today to deny the repellent personal characteristics that marked Heidegger's whole life, including his persistent tendency after the war to lie about his Nazism, his readiness to denounce rivals and out-of-favor colleagues to the Nazi educational hierarchy in order to block their academic advancement, and his callous ingratitude toward all of his early benefactors, especially his principal teacher and patron, Edmund Husserl. By every reliable account, he seems to have been a monstrously self-absorbed man who could bemoan even the most minor personal setbacks to a loyal disciple like Elisabeth Blochmann at the very moment when, as a half-Jew, she was being forced to abandon her academic career and flee Germany. What stands out particularly from all these dismal incidents, though, is the symptomatic disjunction between Heidegger's cautious, personal self-protectiveness and his heroic self-representation. Heidegger casts his thinking in a rhetoric of epochal struggles and decisive turning points. When he uses terms such as "resolution," "boldness," and "daring," it is never entirely clear whether these are intended to denote strictly intellectual traits or qualities of character and temperament, or perhaps both. The rhetoric suggests that there is a link between philosophical and personal "resoluteness" but offers no explanation of how that link arises or functions. There is a note of compensatory self-aggrandizement to Heidegger's rhetoric, an intellectual's longing for the glamour of the combatant who risks his life for a cause. Indeed, part of the seductiveness of Nazism for German intellectuals like Heidegger was its promise to make their theoretical labor part of a militant national renewal. No doubt that same rhetoric helps account for some of Heidegger's continuing appeal to a contemporary professorate whose politics certainly differ from his, but who are eager to regard their own work in similarly dramatic terms.

Like Freud and Wittgenstein, Heidegger was able to endow the very enterprise of thinking with an element of personal, as well as intellectual, risk. At a time of deepening world crisis, when Being itself is in danger of being forgotten, he holds out the hope that a great philosopher may appear, a "hero" who has the charisma to become "a spur for others, so that philosophizing awakens in them" sufficiently to combat the global triumph of technology and nihilism.[30] Heidegger may have dismissed the intellectual pertinence of merely biographical stories about the lives of earlier philosophers, but acquiring the charismatic authority of "*Dasein*'s hero" was central to his own conception of his task. The effort not to appear like an ordinary teacher of philosophy was both instinctive and calculated, and Heidegger looked for ways to endow all of his actions with an aura of the extraordinary and the disruptive. Some of these seem rather comic in their academic competitiveness. In 1922, for example, when he took up a junior position at Marburg, Heidegger scheduled his lectures as early in the morning as possible, not only to test the fidelity of his adherents, but also to force them to chose between his courses and those of the reigning "star" of the philosophy department, Nicolai Hartmann, who kept his students up late into the night in philosophical discussions. Against the bourgeois conventionality of German academic garb, Heidegger liked appearing in his skiing outfit in the winter and in his instantly recognizable, specially designed loden suit and knickerbockers during the summer.[31] His thinking was to be received as an eruption of some primal force, radically different in kind as well as in quality from anything produced by his fellow philosophers. The examples of Kierkegaard and Nietzsche, both of whom wrote their major works in isolation, were crucial to Heidegger, and many of his idiosyncrasies were part of an effort to appropriate the outsider's authenticity of his chosen predecessors while himself remaining securely within the German university establishment. The thrilling rhetoric in which he urged his listeners to admit the "inner terror . . . that every mystery carries with it and that gives *Dasein* its greatness"[32] until the very ground they stand on "is turned into an abyss"[33] belongs to the same constellation of talismanic props as the stylized Swabian peasant outfits, the retreats to his famous cottage at Todtnauberg in the Black Forest, and his deliberately antiquated spelling of central concept words (e.g., *Seyn* for *Sein*). The teacher as well as the teaching must be seen as dwelling in the kind of primal solitude indispensable for the emergence of a redemptively new way of thinking.

For Heidegger, the redemptively new was also the most archaic, a bringing back into the light of forgotten origins and first questions. His favorite term for this kind of thinking was "primordial," and it demanded finding a "path back into the historical foundations of thought . . . to think through questions unasked before or since the Greeks."[34] The ambition to be the most primordial thinker and "preserve the force of the most elementary words" was fundamental for Heidegger and only intensified as he grew older. It is in many ways an odd ambition, especially for someone whose work contains such searching reflections on human temporality and the historicity of Being. Yet the rhetoric of primordiality saturates not only his own texts, but also the descriptions of his most ardent admirers. Here, for example, is how Hannah Arendt praised her former teacher and lover on his eightieth birthday:

> The gale that blows through Heidegger's thinking—like that which
> still, after thousands of years, blows to us from Plato's work—is not of
> our century. It comes from the primordial, and what it leaves behind
> is something perfect which, like everything perfect, falls back into the
> primordial.[35]

It is hard not to be discomfited by praise so overwrought. But to describe Heidegger in terms of a quest for "the primordial" is less eccentric than it first appears. The urge to recapture the intensity and energy of first things, to find in the origins of Western self-understanding new instigations for the present, is one of the twentieth century's dominant imaginative impulses, and its effects are traceable throughout the art and the theorizing of high modernism. One can think here not just of Joyce's *Ulysses*, but also of how Pound begins his *Cantos* with a translation of Book XI of the *Odyssey*, the *Nekyiai*, or descent to the Underworld, which he thought was the oldest portion of Homer's epic. Pound renders Homer's lines into an English metrics derived from alliterative Anglo-Saxon verse. The two primordial origins of English poetry are thus concretely invoked and "made new" at the very outset of Pound's modern verse epic. The passion and richness of "the primordial" is exactly what Joyce and Pound were trying to reach in their texts. Freud, too, thought of himself as founding a new science whose objective was to find a way back to the primordial, all-explaining origin, initially of an individual's psyche, and later, in works such as *Beyond the Pleasure Principle* (1920) and *Civilization and Its Discontents* (1929–30), of human culture as a whole.

Although Heidegger despised modernism in all its manifestations and summarily dismissed modern literature as "predominantly destructive,"[36] his 1927 *Being and Time* is a perfect example of the "modernist masterpiece" described in the introduction. *Being and Time* appeared in the same decade as *Ulysses,* the first sections of the *Cantos,* Rilke's *Duino Elegies,* Wittgenstein's *Tractatus Logico-Philosophicus,* Alban Berg's *Wozzeck,* much of Proust's *Remembrance of Things Past,* and several of the major texts in Freud's *Standard Edition.* Like them, *Being and Time* explicitly presents itself as both the culmination of a lengthy tradition and a radical departure from its predecessors. In its enormous, deliberate difficulty, its desire to address the most decisive, fundamental questions, its internal self-referentiality, and its encouragement of an attitude of discipleship among its readers, *Being and Time* embodies all the defining characteristics of a modernist masterpiece. It is particularly ironic that a text so often misread as an antimodernist manifesto—including, most insistently, by its own author—should, in fact, be an absolutely characteristic product of high modernism at its most ambitious. Its title already makes clear the extent of its aim: in this book, the foundations of our entire existence are at stake. Its prologue admonishes us that we have forgotten what Being is, and we have even forgotten this forgetting, so that the task ahead, like Proust's or Freud's, is to tell the story of an abysmal loss and the immensely difficult struggle of recapturing what has been forgotten. Like Joyce and Rilke among his near contemporaries, or like Paul Celan in the next generation, Heidegger flaunts a dazzling set of word coinings and new concepts, reinventing philosophical prose at the level of the individual syllable as well as of the whole paragraph and chapter. Most important, *Being and Time,* like all of Heidegger's central texts, and like many of the main modernist masterpieces, is a continuous affirmation of the power of the exceptional instant with a corresponding contempt for the insignificance, indeed even the perniciousness, of such prosaic longings as personal happiness or social amelioration.[37] What matters are the moments of ecstatic rupture, the shattering of the quotidian rhythms and banal regularities of ordinary human existence. We are thrown into a world of others, but their speech is the idle chatter, the *Gerede,* in which our authenticity is drowned. Amid their babbling, we no longer even notice that Being itself has been silenced.

"Being-lost into They"[38] is Heidegger's chilling description of routinized social existence in which whatever becomes public is necessarily degraded because a plurality of voices reduces hierarchic truth to mere opinion. "Publicness," he writes, "is insensitive to every difference of level and of genuineness."[39] Most of our existence is spent in a publicness that is really a fundamental self-alienation, a life "living out of itself" for which Heidegger coins the term "ruinance" (*Ruinanz*), with its implications of a catastrophic fall into inauthenticity and forgetfulness. Although he explicitly tried to deny their theological provenance, the language of fallenness and the idea that "factual life" is nothing but a continuous falling away from the plenitude of Being bear clear traces of Heidegger's former religious studies. But now it is up to the thinker and poet, not the priest, to awaken us to our dire situation. In such an awakening, there is no rescue from the fall, no ultimate redemption or link to a timeless eternity; there is only a heightened awareness of our own time-bound and care-riddled existence. As with Proustian recollection, the grounding faith in *Being and Time* is that when we truly awaken to an understanding of our transience and contingency, the facts of our existence will not have changed in any externally noticeable way, but our inner stance toward them will be utterly transformed. For Heidegger, philosophy begins when we are courageous enough to open ourselves to the primordial Nothingness (*das Nichts*) and through that encounter allow the question of *Dasein* to arise for us in all its richness and dread. As he puts it in "What Is Metaphysics?" his 1929 inaugural lecture as Husserl's successor to the chair of philosophy at Freiburg, "Only on the ground of the original relation of the nothing can human existence approach and penetrate beings. . . . Dasein means: being held out into the nothing."[40] Like Wallace Stevens's Snow Man, the resolute Heideggerian consciousness learns to stand in the midst of existence without requiring any further consolation or transcendence than the unfathomable mystery of its own being in the midst of the circumambient nothingness:

> And, nothing himself, beholds
> Nothing that is not there and the nothing that is.[41]

A complex network of interrelated binary oppositions structures Heidegger's texts: the division between authentic and inauthentic existence, between the single, resolute human being and the anonymous "They" who make up the public realm, between the "ready-to-hand" disinterested, impersonal way of relating to the world and the "present-at-hand" vital and meaning-filled way of doing so, between Time experienced as resolution, anxiety, and care versus Time experienced as mere mechanical succession. The famous existential analysis of *Dasein* is always pitched *in extremis* because that is viewed as the only possible mode for a meaningful life. In *Being and Time*, it is *Angst* (translated as "anxiety" by Macquarrie and Robinson, although "dread," in Kierkegaard's sense, would be more accurate) rather than joy or desire or even love that awakens us to ask about the meaning of *Dasein*. For Heidegger, to possess the "courage for anxiety"[42] is the first and most important step toward experiencing ourselves and the world authentically; and in comparison with so compelling a task, ordinary human needs or moral distinctions lose their significance.

What is so haunting about this aspect of Heidegger's thinking is how entirely he turned his back on the most promising directions his own work had initially opened up. *Being and Time* contains a critique of the objectivization (*Vergegenständlichung*) of our ordinary lived experience that is unparalleled in any other philosopher of the twentieth century. Heidegger shows how the rejection of the everyday world and the insistence on a transcendental foundation for one's beliefs "de-experiences" experience and "de-worlds" the world as we actually encounter it. In the hands of someone less enthralled by the revelatory power of the extreme, these arguments might have led to a philosophically rich comprehension of the value of the prosaic. For unlike logicians or ordinary language philosophers, Heidegger wants to analyze words by taking into account their historicity, not just their immediate—and transitory—usage. He seeks to restore to language its proper historical density and to give pretheoretical experience its proper attention and value. But his dismissal of the worth of an "inauthentic" life is perfectly mirrored in his lack of interest in any use of language except by one of his constellation of geniuses. His disregard for the communal, collectively acquired meaning of words vitiates the theoretical and ethical advantage that his acute historical awareness might have provided. For Heidegger, it is only how Heraclitus and Sophocles, or Nietzsche and Hölderlin, used words that is of interest, not the language as it was employed by the inhabitants of a classical Greek polis or by ordinary nineteenth-century Germans. To Heidegger, the idea that the community of speech users throughout the culture's linguistic history has helped shape the words that the great poets employ is an irrelevance. Quite the contrary: for Heidegger, the community as such has nothing substantive to contribute to the poet's words, since it is these poet-seers, and they alone, who create "the essential disposition [*Grundstimmung*], that is, the truth of the *Dasein* of a *Volk*."[43]

In a strong sense, Heidegger implies that there is really no reason why anyone except the great poet and his philosopher-explicator should speak at all. Since their words already contain everything of value in the culture, the addition of lesser voices would only drown out the plenitude of the original utterance. The great thinkers and poets speak to and for one another from the solitary heights of their genius, and their speech is what Heidegger will call the history of Being. The number of nonphilosophers Heidegger regards as participating in this conversation is astonishingly small: no musicians are included at all, only Van Gogh among painters, scarcely any prose fiction writers, and barely half a dozen poets. Yet perhaps because of the narrowness of his imaginative range, Heidegger listens to the few voices he venerates with an often exemplary attentiveness. No philosopher, not even Nietzsche, has ever devoted more exegetical brilliance to analyzing the philosophical significance of poetry. Heidegger's relationship to poetry is unique in Western philosophy. When other philosophers cite literary texts at all, they almost invariably do so for the purpose of illustration, or to find a more elegant way of stating ideas they have already formulated independently. There is no suggestion that the work of art itself has fundamentally helped determine the direction of their philosophical argument. For Heidegger, however, the words of the poets are not merely illustrative, they are actually generative of his ideas. But for all the conceptual richness and the moments of genuine illumination, Heidegger's dialogue with his chosen poet and thinker is a conversation from which the rest of us are categorically excluded. Finally, this self-enclosedness makes even the most searching speech shrill.

In *Being and Time*, Heidegger still cared not only about the intensification but also about the clarification of *Dasein*. He was willing to devote an important section of the book to the function of signs—including such quotidian, unheraldic examples as a car's turn signal—as part of the process of disclosing *Dasein*, and he acknowledges that the sense of *Dasein* can even be fructified by the everyday chatter of *Gerede*, if only because the limitations of that condition are among the first ways a desire for something deeper and more authentic is awakened.[44] But in 1929, at a famous colloquium in Davos, Switzerland, two years after *Being and Time* had confirmed his preeminence in German philosophy, Heidegger engaged in a widely followed public debate with Ernst Cassirer. Cassirer represented the kind of cosmopolitan humanism Heidegger despised, and it was against the beleaguered liberal tradition in European thought, already under siege throughout the Continent, that Heidegger proclaimed, "Man exists at the peak of his own possibilities only at a very few moments."[45] And only a very few men, he went on to argue, have the inner resolution to welcome those moments. If Heidegger's earlier writings still addressed concerns shared by ordinary human beings, after the Davos encounter, Heidegger's work increasingly restricted itself to a meditation on the rare thinkers and poets whose texts are a record of their existence at those peak moments. With the rest of humankind, he will, for the most part, no longer seriously concern himself. The longing for security and contentment felt by the masses is regarded by Heidegger as just another sinister symptom of a global, unheeded catastrophe, the *Seinsvergessenheit*, or forgetfulness-of-Being, that has become so rooted it may no longer be reversible. Even his teaching, in which Heidegger had always taken a certain pride, seems to have started mattering less. Indeed, he begins to think of himself neither as a teacher nor as a philosopher engaged in a dialogue with his students and colleagues, but, more grandiosely and self-dramatizingly, as a man caught up in "a conversation of essential thinking with itself."[46]

From now on, it is solely the intensification of the sense of *Dasein* that will continue to matter to Heidegger. Nothing shows more clearly his deep roots in German Romanticism than this absolute privileging of intensity. Already in 1756, Johann Georg Hamann had proclaimed: "Do either nothing or everything; the mediocre, the moderate, is repellent to me: I prefer an extreme,"[47] and Heidegger's schism between authentic and inauthentic existence is only the most seductive philosophical elaboration of the antiprosaic dictates of the Romantic counter-Enlightenment merged with a Rousseauistic loathing of the triviality of everyday social discourse and desires. A messianic leader like Hitler, who claimed to incarnate the inwardness and authenticity of the entire German people and who promised to mobilize the whole *Volk* for a great, world-transforming mission, drew upon the same charged romantic themes. The fact that Nazism won Heidegger's temporary allegiance is not particularly surprising, especially since its celebration of the moment of crisis as the true test of an individual and a people, its emphasis on the charismatic authority of the single genius, and its loathing for the "idle chatter" of parliamentarians all appeared to echo some of his own long-held convictions. And yet, the moral limitations of his thinking are apparent independently of the particular political movement in which he, for whatever length of time, placed his hopes. From the beginning, Heidegger's thinking was profoundly antidemocratic, and in one of his central texts, *What Is Called Thinking?* he makes clear that concern for social betterment is utterly irrelevant to the far more urgent question of *Dasein*'s "ruinance": "the devastation . . . can easily go hand in hand with a guaranteed supreme living standard for man, and just as easily with the organized establishment of a uniform state of happiness for all men."[48] Precisely by making the welfare of its citizens a society's raison d'être, liberal democracy is inherently hostile to a Heideggerian concern for the fate of Being. Had there been no Third Reich, or had Heidegger never spoken a word championing it, Heideggerian philosophy would be just as vulnerable to an ethical critique. This criticism was succinctly articulated by the late historian of ideas Amos Funkenstein. He premised his objection to Heidegger on the prosaicist assumption that "human life and the incommensurable value of each individual" must be regarded as absolute. "From an ethical point of view," Funkenstein observed, "every life is authentic, a value in and of itself, not interchangeable with any other human life, a mode *sui generis*." But respecting "the integrity and worthiness of each concrete individual life, however lived"[49] requires that one reject the fundamental Heideggerian notion of an unbridgeable chasm between authentic and inauthentic life, and the attendant belief that it is only the experience of a crisis that "calls man to his true self." Thus, a rigorous criticism of Heidegger's thinking need not base itself upon his explicit political allegiances at all. It is by regarding the undramatic, quotidian moments of lived experience as significant in their own right, and not merely as symptoms of "ruinance" and "boredom," that one challenges his philosophy at its core. The very possibility that an ordinary life lived in ordinary circumstances might have its own integrity and worth is precisely what Heidegger's thinking precludes. He defines an authentic existence in such a way as to banish from it most actual forms and practices of human conduct, effectively delegitimizing almost all individual lives by excluding them from the only history that matters: that of Being itself.

Contrary to the basic insight of *Being and Time* that the emergence and conceal-
ment of *Dasein* is a temporal process, Heidegger more typically characterizes its
advent as a unique moment of apotheosis, ecstasy, and epiphany, best expressed in
his own distinctively elevated, hieratic, and ceremonially repetitive language. Real
human existence could be thought of as almost the exact inverse of Heideggerian
Dasein, and it is the defense of that unheroic, heterogeneous life, the texture and
rhythm of our daily routines and decisions with their myriad of small, unspectacular
adjustments offered in the interest of a habitable social world, that is the real answer
to Heidegger's fascination with the glamour of daring and authenticity.

Heidegger's Nazism was neither strictly entailed by his philosophy nor merely
accidental to it. Instead, the relationship hovers between these poles in a way that
can be thought of as a kind of eerie parallelism. Nothing in Heidegger's philosophy
was derived from Nazism, and there is much in it that is inimical to Nazi beliefs.
But at its core there is also a constellation of assumptions about what is valuable and
what is dross in human existence whose similarity to the apocalyptic and messianic
strains in Nazism seems incontestable. Heidegger's loathing for modern life made
him seek a political solution in a movement whose leadership had no interest in him
except as a propagandist on whose prestige they could draw. But what he shared
with them was a contempt for pluralism, diversity, multiplicity, and heterogeneity.
For Heidegger, truth, whether or not it is heeded, remains single and uniform. The
tripartite Nazi slogan, "*Ein* Volk, *Ein* Reich, und *Ein* Führer" (one people, one empire,
and one leader), is simply the vulgar and demagogic manifestation of an analogous
urge to subsume the multifariousness of political life into a single mythic unity.
The myth of the *Volk* was so appealing to Heidegger, not because he ever shared
the biological racism at the basis of Nazi ideology, but because the hypothesis of a
single race and nation let him speak to and about a collectivity in terms that really
apply only to individuals. Only the oxymoron of a collective singularity like the
Volk can be judged in terms of "authenticity" or "inauthenticity"—categories that
otherwise make little sense about communities of different human beings. Hence,
too, Heidegger's attraction in the first years of the Third Reich to the historically
and logically bizarre notion of a national fundamental ontology, expressed in the
metamorphosis of *Je-meinigkeit* (mineness) into *Je-unsrigkeit* (ourness).[50] Being calls
us, for Heidegger, though we have largely lost both the will and the capacity to
heed it. But it calls us with one voice, to one task, and in one language (German).
It is unthinkable to Heidegger that Being can speak in many accents, including
even the vernacular of the modern consciousness.

Heidegger disliked Descartes and saw himself as deconstructing the metaphysical tradition out of which Descartes arose. His celebrated dissatisfaction with
parts of *Being and Time*, for example, arose because he felt that its language was still
too metaphysical and thus distorted his new conception of Being. As his thinking
progressed, Heidegger began to use some of that book's central terms, notably

Dasein itself, less and less. He let it be known, often through gnomic asides and brief hints, that his thought had turned decisively away from any conception of Being, language, and existence that was still dependent on the metaphysics latent in *Being and Time*. Thus, in the 1947 "Letter on Humanism," Heidegger explains that he "held back" the third section of part 1 of *Being and Time* because his thinking "failed in the adequate saying of this turning [*Kehre*] and did not succeed with the help of the language of metaphysics."[51] And, no doubt, since he interpreted the term "metaphysical" as meaning the acceptance of the traditional dichotomy between subject and object, there was indeed a compelling need to find a new way of formulating a challenge to that dichotomy. In this project, Heidegger is not so far from Musil's dissatisfaction with the traditional metaphysical conception of subjectivity or from Rilke's more intuitive rejection of the boundaries between absolute inwardness and the entirety of creation. Yet Heidegger's lifelong emphasis on the linguistic and cultural singularity of Being's self-revelation is closer to a metaphysical quest for certainty than to any essayistic, provisional acceptance of multiplicity. Indeed, among the most puzzling contradictions in Heidegger is that while he regularly insists that his thinking rejects the lure of an absolute, transcendent truth (the metaphysical concept par excellence), so many of his basic categories and terms imply the very transcendent certainty he claims to do without. As Heidegger's interpreters have repeatedly pointed out, in his thinking, human beings do not discover a truth existing independently outside them: they live within an interpretative horizon—different in each epoch—in which the world is given a certain shape, meaning, and terminology.[52] But if this is so, then on what basis can Heidegger regard the Greek, and subsequently the German, stance toward Being and the world as superior to any other? And, analogously, how can he judge the modern relationship to Being as inherently worse than the stance of earlier eras? His charged term "truth-happening" (*Wahrheitsgeschehen*), which he opposes to the Platonic notion of a transcendent, immutable truth, suggests a temporal, unfolding process, but increasingly, Heidegger discards any implication of process at all, preferring instead to picture authentic thinking in images of an unmoving, adamantine fixity, as in the famous declaration that "to think is to confine yourself to a single thought that one day stands still like a star in the world's sky."[53] (Here, the largely unrecognized influence of Kierkegaard's *Purity of Heart Is to Will One Thing* can be clearly heard.) Nothing is less Montaigne-like, less open to an essayistic acceptance that there may be, and indeed usually are, conflicting, mutually exclusive ideas, practices, beliefs, and values, each of which is legitimate in its own way and among which a human being must negotiate in an ongoing series of local choices and judgments, without an overarching permanent hierarchy to which one can always appeal for a resolution. In Heidegger's interpretation, almost everything that actually occurs in the life of an individual or a community is a hindrance to the self-revelation of Being, and the privileged sites in which such an epiphany can occur are more and more narrowly defined. The Black Forest becomes Heidegger's Duino Castle: nowhere else can the radiance of Being manifest itself so fully. Heidegger's metaphysically resonant mourning for the growing devastation that modernity has inflicted on Being entails a profound hostility to the modern city and to the promiscuous mingling of peoples, voices, and activities that urban life has fostered. He envelops the call of Being in a litany of Romantic nature imagery (the forest clearing, the plowed field, the lonely path through the forest) intended to convey timelessness, stability, and rootedness, but whose cumulative effect comes dangerously close to kitsch. Here, for example, is a passage from a famous broadcast lecture of March 1934, "Creative Landscape: Why Do We Stay in the Province?" in which Heidegger explained his reasons for rejecting the offer of a chair in Berlin:

> Recently I got a second invitation to teach at the University of Berlin. On that occasion I left Freiburg and withdrew to the cabin. I listened to what the mountains and the forest and the farmlands were saying, and I went to see an old friend of mine, a 75-year-old farmer. He had read about the call to Berlin in the newspaper. What could he say? Slowly he fixed the sure gaze of his clear eyes on mine, and keeping his mouth tightly shut, he thoughtfully put his faithful hand on my shoulder. Ever so slightly he shook his head. That meant: absolutely no.[54]

The same unpleasantly *völkisch* sentimentalization of the provincial and the peasantlike as the privileged source of abiding value is not confined to his secondary speeches and texts. It marks many of Heidegger's central reflections in the period after *Being and Time*, including such fundamental meditations as "The Origin of the Work of Art." This is one of the few places where Heidegger draws upon a painting, Van Gogh's stark portrait of a pair of worn peasant shoes (*Old Shoes with Laces*), rather than a poem, to exemplify his point about the place of homespun artifacts, of labor and land, and blood and soil, in the network of meaning through which a world is articulated:

> From the dark opening of the worn insides of the shoes the toilsome tread of the worker stares forth. In the stiffly rugged heaviness of the shoes there is the accumulated tenacity of her slow trudge through the far-spreading and ever-uniform furrows of the field swept by a raw wind. On the leather lie the dampness and richness of the soil. Under the soles slides the loneliness of the field-path as evening falls. In the shoes vibrates the silent call of the earth, its quiet gift of the ripening grain and its unexplained self-refusal in the fallow desolation of the wintry field. This equipment is pervaded by uncomplaining anxiety as to the certainty of bread, the

wordless joy of having once more withstood want, the trembling before the impending childbed, and shivering at the surrounding menace of death. This equipment belongs to the *earth* and it is protected in the *world* of the peasant woman. From out of this protected belonging, the equipment itself rises to its resting-within-itself.[55]

At the end of his extended prose ekphrasis, Heidegger explicitly announces, "The art work lets us know what shoes are in truth."[56] A few years after these absolute declarations of Heidegger's, Meyer Schapiro would prove that the shoes in question were Van Gogh's own and not a peasant woman's at all. Schapiro's essay is devastating about the sentimental projections that replace any real scrutiny of the painting in Heidegger's account:

> Alas, for him, the philosopher has indeed deceived himself. He has retained from his encounter with Van Gogh's canvas a moving set of associations with peasants and the soil, which are not sustained by the picture itself but are grounded rather in his own social outlook with its heavy pathos of the primordial and earthy. . . . he has experienced both too little and too much in his contact with the work. The error lies not only in his projection which replaces a close and true attention to the work of art. For even if he had seen a picture of a peasant woman's shoes as he describes them, it would be a mistake to suppose that the truth he uncovered in the painting—the being of the shoes—is something given here once and for all . . . I find nothing in Heidegger's fanciful description . . . that could not have been imagined in looking at a real pair of peasants' shoes.[57]

Schapiro, of course, limits himself to the art-historical misinterpretations that determine Heidegger's essay and avoids any general critique of the philosopher's rhetoric in his other texts. But Thomas Bernhard, Austria's greatest postwar novelist and playwright, who was probably familiar with Schapiro's critique, shows no hesitation in registering an overall judgment of Heidegger's prose as well as of his ideas. Bernhard is one of the few writers to have focused directly on the element of kitsch in Heidegger's language and his self-representation. Bernhard's 1985 novel *Old Masters* contains an extended and wickedly funny diatribe against Heidegger, the self-crowned lonely sage of Todtnauberg, in whom Bernhard finds the incarnation of "that ridiculous Nazi philistinism . . . [that has] kitschified philosophy."[58] Heidegger's rhetoric, with its mixture of provincial pietism and preindustrial nostalgia, substitutes pathos for ethos and in the process blurs the distinctions that might lend his critique of modernity a less compromised reso-nance. Musil's notion of "the subjunctive of possibility," the essayistic realization, discussed in the previous chapter, that everything in the world could "just as well be done differently," is simply unthinkable in Heideggerian terms. In his philosophy, history, thought, and the gradually dimming hope for Being's self-disclosure all follow a melancholy downward trajectory devoid of any meaningful alternatives or sideshadows. Heidegger's nostalgia marks him as Europe's last, unwavering metaphysician of calamity, not as a guide to a new thinking beyond the dead end of an alienating dualism. In the now famous interview conducted with the editors of *Der Spiegel* in 1966 but, at his instructions, published posthumously, Heidegger announced that the darkness of modernity and nihilism had spread over the globe so forcefully that now "only a God can save us." Perhaps so, but not a God that Heidegger himself would have recognized or welcomed.

4

Walter Benjamin
Apocalypse and Memory

In September 1915, the journal *Der neue Merkur* published an essay on "The Life of Students" by Walter Benedix Schönflies Benjamin, a twenty-three-year-old university student from a prosperous and thoroughly assimilated Jewish family in Berlin. In the years before the outbreak of World War I, the German Youth Movement had succeeded in attracting widespread attention to its demands for educational reform and "spiritual renewal," and some of its leaders, including Gustav Wyneken, Benjamin's former mentor, had become controversial, nationally known public figures. But even in the charged atmosphere of the day, it is unlikely that the journal's readers were prepared for this young man's hieratic tone, or the sweeping self-confidence of his assertions. Here is how "The Life of Students" opens:

> There is a conception of history that puts its faith in the infinite extent of time and thus distinguishes only the speed, or lack of it, with which people and epochs advance along the path of progress. This corresponds to a certain lack of context, want of precision, and strictness of demand, which this conception places on the present. The following remarks, in contrast, consider a definite condition in which history appears to be concentrated into a single focal point, like those traditionally found in the utopian images of the thinkers. The elements of the ultimate condition do not manifest themselves as a formless tendency toward progress, but rather are deeply rooted in every present as the most endangered, most disparaged and derided creations and thoughts. The historical task is to disclose this immanent state of perfection and make it absolute, to make it visible and dominant in the present. This condition cannot be delineated through a pragmatic description of details (the history of institutions, customs, and so on) . . . it can only be grasped in its metaphysical structure, as with the Messianic Kingdom or the idea of the French Revolution. It is worth taking

the trouble to describe the contemporary historical significance of students and the university . . . only if they can be understood as a metaphor, as an image of the highest metaphysical state of history. . . . all that remains is to consciously liberate the future from its deformations in the present. This is criticism's sole task.[1]

By the time this text appeared in print, its author had already acquired a certain reputation for earnest, bookish intensity. In spite of his prickly fastidiousness, he was a recognized figure in the student movement and was twice elected president of the Free Students' Association at the Friedrich Wilhelm University in Berlin. Indeed, a few months earlier, in June 1915, he had presented some of the central ideas from "The Life of Students" as part of a lengthy intervention at a public discussion also attended by Gerhard (later Gershom) Scholem, who had just turned eighteen, and who testified, decades later, to the powerful impression that Benjamin made on people. Scholem gives a wonderful description of a still earlier speech that Benjamin delivered on the question of how German Jews should relate to their dual heritage. In the autumn of 1913, Scholem writes, Benjamin addressed a joint meeting of Jung Juda, the Berlin Zionist youth organization, and Wyneken's Youth Movement, of which Benjamin was "rumored to be the most gifted intellect." Benjamin "made a very tortuous speech in which he did not reject Zionism outright but somehow relegated it to a secondary position. Without looking at the audience, he delivered his absolutely letter-perfect speech with great intensity to an upper corner of the ceiling, at which he stared the whole time." The speech, which has not been preserved, was no doubt as "tortuous" as Scholem recalls, but it was also sufficiently powerful to make Scholem end his account by admitting, "I do not recall the rejoinder made by the Zionists."[2]

Indeed, for all their occasionally clotted syntax and conceptual opacity, the questions taken up in Benjamin's first essays, whether in unpublished pieces like "The Metaphysics of Youth" (written 1913–14) and "Two Poems by Friedrich Hölderlin" (written 1914–15), or in printed texts like "The Life of Students," are remarkably consonant with his mature concerns, and reading these prewar pieces confirms how dubious is the conventional division of his thinking into discrete phases. Though they flaunt the scholasticism of the library and the self-entangling jargon of the philosophical debating society, it is not so much the theoretical "difficulty" of Benjamin's early works that sometimes makes them so off-putting, but rather their bewildering combination of probing, original insights and embarrassing commonplaces, all cloaked in the identical rhetoric of labyrinthine abstraction. Every phrase seems burdened with the pressure of never articulating anything less than an all-encompassing, categorical perception, and whole paragraphs palpably buckle under the strain. Clearly this subterranean instability beneath an intransigently confident surface cannot be explained away as just the inevitable, self-regarding tics of a brilliant young man trying to compel the applause he professes to disdain. The same unsteadiness of aim resonates just as troublingly in much of Benjamin's mature work and helps explain why so many of his projects remained incomplete.

Even a slight essay like "The Life of Students" is already dense with the specific preoccupations—and even some of the vital formulations—that would obsess Benjamin throughout his life. Most strikingly, there is the insistence on two radically incommensurate conceptions of history: the first, which Benjamin evokes only to dismiss entirely, is gradualist, evolutionary, and unsystematic; the second is utopian, absolutist, and metaphysical, and it commands all of Benjamin's passionate allegiance. For him, it is solely the exceptional events, the apocalyptic moments, that matter. Only they contain sufficient depth of meaning to illuminate the present. What Benjamin will later call "homogeneous time,"[3] that is, time as continuous duration, is empty of significance. The sole way of seizing the inner truth of one's own historical moment is to focus on the disruptive and singular aspects revealed by history and metaphysics. It follows from such an assumption that any attempt to ameliorate the present by piecemeal reform is trivial and even dangerous, since nothing short of an all-encompassing transformation, the bringing to fruition of an "immanent state of perfection," makes any significant difference. For the intellectual, the only legitimate task is to fashion something like a metaphysical still life, a crystallization in which history itself, as a kind of absolute, hypostatized subject, is suddenly made visible, "concentrated into a single focal point . . . [like] in the utopian images of the thinkers." As in his invocation of "the *idea* of French Revolution," Benjamin is willing to take seriously only the distilled theoretical residue of an occurrence, not any messily concrete course of events. It is solely as an image of the messianic kingdom that the French Revolution matters to Benjamin, and though the locus and terms of that utopian messianism will change many times throughout Benjamin's life, the search for it remained his most abiding intellectual and emotional commitment.

Each one of these sentences from 1915 could just as easily have been heard at a philosophical seminar in any German university in 1810. It is the language of Schelling, Schlegel, Novalis, and Fichte that gives Benjamin his central tropes, and it is the metaphysical imperatives of German Idealism that determine his arguments, not the situation of an imperiled student body, many of whose members were soon to face annihilation in the mass slaughter of the First World War. The reality of that war was already fundamentally transforming every aspect of German life and society, especially that of its youth. It would soon make Benjamin himself break completely with Wyneken and move to Switzerland to continue his studies, but it is scarcely registered at all in this essay about "The Life of Students." There is something both admirable and profoundly disturbing about Benjamin's refusal to allow the direction of his reflections to be affected by either his own or his listeners' immediate circumstances. It is a characteristic that will mark Benjamin's thinking throughout his life, even—or, more accurately, particularly—when he himself is in danger, and it is impossible for an outsider to separate the courage from the folly in his decisions. What seems to intensify during the 1930s, though, is his almost Simone Weil–like refusal of prudential concern for his own welfare when doing so might jeopardize one of his literary-philosophical projects. But Benjamin never stopped trying to add some denser, more humanly compelling content to his yearning for what he often had no way to designate except by the vague phrase "the Messianic Kingdom," and a great deal of polemical energy has been expended in the attempt to sort out the Jewish from the Marxist provenance in his messianic thinking. His early writings strongly suggest, however, that these may be idle battles. No doubt, Scholem's tutelage helped lend Benjamin's apocalyptic images a Jewish tinge,[4] just as his Bolshevik lover, the Latvian theater and film figure Asja Lacis, initiated him into the fantasies of an emancipatory Marxism. Lacis, replaced a few years later by the still more powerful example of Bertolt Brecht, taught Benjamin to update his idea of the French Revolution with that of the 1917 Russian one, but it is clear that the category of a messianic redemption of history was central to Benjamin long before Scholem, Lacis, or Brecht ever crossed his path. It was from the problematic legacy of Germanic-Christian mysticism, especially as it was sublimated and redirected toward literary-philosophical speculation in the work of the Jena Romantics, that Benjamin first drew his image of messianic redemption, and that heritage remains clearly audible across all of his subsequent intellectual transformations.

The continuity in Benjamin's thinking is remarkable, and it is nowhere more evident than in the contempt with which all of his writings treat not merely the possibility, but even the value of any gradual, piecemeal improvement in social conditions. From the opening sentence of "The Life of Students" to his last text, the celebrated "Theses on the Philosophy of History," which he completed in the spring of 1940, it is impossible for Benjamin to mention the word "progress" without derision. To him, the notion of "progress" is simply the last refuge of the intellectually philistine and the politically corrupt. Indeed, of all the policies that the German Communist Party adopted at Stalin's command, the only one that won Benjamin's unwavering allegiance was the definition of the Social Democrats, rather than the Fascist and Nazi parties, as the real enemy of humankind. Moreover, Benjamin actually went much further in his rejection of left-liberal gradualism than anything mandated by communist solidarity. In an amalgam that clearly owed more to his lifelong personal preoccupations than to Marxist doctrine, Benjamin became convinced that Social Democratic policies, old-fashioned narrative historiography, and a belief in the attainability of social progress were in fact three directly linked manifestations of a single evil. In his view, it was precisely these three ideas that had prepared the philosophical path for fascism's success, and each of them needed to be categorically resisted. It is difficult to imagine a more disastrously self-isolating position in the embattled circumstances of the 1930s, but Benjamin clung to it with increasing stubbornness, even as its untenability became more evident with every Nazi victory. In fact, despite his frequent references to contemporary events, politics as part of daily, collective life was largely irrelevant to Benjamin's theorizing. Such is usually the case with messianic absolutism, but rarely has the abyss between historical events as they are actually unfolding and the framework of ideas used to explain them seemed deeper or more unbridgeable than in Benjamin's speculations.

Written as the Nazi armies were already overrunning France, Benjamin's "Theses on the Philosophy of History" sought to safeguard the promise that a messianic redemption is equally possible at any moment in history. Considering that when he wrote these theses it was the permanent enslavement of Europe and the extermination of its Jews that looked far more likely, there is a certain heroic obduracy to Benjamin's ending his text with the affirmation that at least for the Jews, "every second of time was the strait gate through which the Messiah might enter."[5] Throughout the "Theses," Benjamin attempts an uneasy conflation of Marxist and Jewish terminologies, just as, in his earlier theorizing championing avant-garde art and writing, he had sought to integrate the transgressive promises of the communist and the surrealist *Manifestos.* But whether the language of redemption is couched in theological, materialist, or strictly poetic-psychological tropes, it is clearly of secondary importance: all that truly matters is to remain vigilant for the manifestation of the messianic in all its guises.

Benjamin was mesmerized by historical ruptures, malignant or beneficent, literary or political, because he was convinced of the revelatory authority of the unique and the excessive over the typical and the quotidian. He was deeply attracted to a cluster of powerful image ideas in Judaism, but for him these were completely detached from their original context in Jewish collective experience and religious practice. Similarly, as everyone from Asja Lacis to Theodor Adorno quickly saw, his Marxism was a strategic appropriation of a network of charged phrases and concepts to which he was already favorably predisposed, rather than the embracing of a coherent, totalizing system. At their root, the political theories with which Benjamin's real affinities lay were actually those of Marx's great anarchic and syndicalist antagonists, Auguste Blanqui and Mikhail Bakunin. Significantly, in his 1929 essay on surrealism, it is not Marx or Lenin but Bakunin whom Benjamin holds up as the exemplary model who gave Europe its last "radical concept of freedom,"[6] and in the "Theses on the Philosophy of History," the real, if only partially acknowledged, guiding political dream is the Blanquist vision of a surprise insurrection, a sudden, all-transforming seizure of power. No conception of history as an unfolding, time-bound process, whether interpreted in Marxist terms or not, could ever fascinate Benjamin as powerfully as a spontaneous, visionary model. What Benjamin looked for in both his political and his theological sources was the identical privileging of the apocalyptic over the prosaic and the celebration of the moment of crisis as the potential bearer of a messianic revelation.

What is striking in all this, however, is how little Benjamin writes about the actual nature of the messianic kingdom whose possible nearness he never ceases to stress. Few men have written so much about the need for an apocalyptic upheaval and so little about what the messianic kingdom will be like and how humanity will be better off once it has been achieved. The radical asymmetry between Benjamin's detailed evocation of a degraded present and his complete blankness about the redeemed future has, I think, two crucial causes. The first is his recognition that his messianic dream is essentially indifferent to such banal concerns as the material conditions of daily existence. In the "Theologico-Political Fragment," he even admits that "the quest of free humanity for happiness runs counter to the direction of Messianic intensity,"[7] and no amount of dialectical maneuvering can hope to resolve this fundamental antinomy. Indeed, the fragment shows a profound hostility to the impulses that have been indispensable for every mass political movement, and it would fit better among the aphorisms of a great counterrevolutionary thinker like Joseph de Maistre or a poet-dandy like Baudelaire than in the writings of a left-wing radical. Ordinary human happiness is not just irrelevant to Benjamin's messianic longing, it is both its logical antithesis and its greatest practical obstacle, because it threatens to reconcile people to the world as it actually is rather than goading them toward some cataclysmic transfiguration. Put less metaphysically, misery is more conducive to a rejection of the existing order than is contentment. The potentially sinister implications of a reflection like this are clear, even if Benjamin veered away from fully articulating them. But his attacks on social democracy as potentially more dangerous than Nazism and his profound loathing for gradualism in all its forms owe a great deal to the underlying logic of such "theologico-political" premises.

More curious still, though, is the fact that the messianic redemption for which Benjamin longs is fundamentally not oriented toward the future at all. It is the *past*, not the future, that Benjamin's messiah has come to make whole, and in many ways this radical reversal of the topos is the most original, as well as the most fantastical, of all Benjamin's ideas. The face of his angel of history "is turned toward the past"[8] because *there* is where his real desires and his real tasks are rooted. This is an apocalypse of the library and collector's cabinet, not of the streets and factories. If Benjamin's redemptive angel has a historical mission, it is much closer to Marcel Proust's quest to recapture the plenitude of lost time than to Marx's dream of a communist paradise or the future-directed apocalyptic prophecies of Jewish messianism. Repeatedly, it is the retroactive risks to the past from the barbarism of the present that Benjamin's writings emphasize, not the misery inflicted on people in his own time. He insists that "even the dead will not be safe from the enemy if he wins,"[9] and it often seems that he cares more for the welfare of the dead than for that of the living. Benjamin's messianic revolutionary seeks to "fan the spark of hope in the past"[10] not so much in order to light a fire in the present, but because it is in the past that paradise can be found, and it is there that the truly crucial battles are still to be fought. Above all, redemption for Benjamin means making "time come to a stop" and finally stilling the idiot wind "we call progress."[11]

Benjamin was an incomparable reader of authors in whom he sensed kindred elements, and nothing is more revealing of the profound connection between his own rejection of time-as-duration and the backward-turning gaze of his angel of history than the following passage in which Benjamin directly links Baudelaire's and Proust's experiences of temporality:

> Proust writes: "Time is peculiarly chopped up in Baudelaire; only a very few days open up, they are significant ones." . . . These significant days are days of completing Time . . . They are days of recollection not marked by any experience. They are not connected with other days but stand out from Time.[12]

Days of recollection, unmarked by any new experiences or events, are what most deeply attract Benjamin and come closest to his sense of what a fully redeemed time would be like. Little wonder that Asja Lacis quickly despaired of converting Benjamin into a plausible Marxist. More seriously troubling, though, is Benjamin's fantasy that a redemptive transformation in the present will make good everything that was left incomplete and injured in the past. As a theological hope grounded in the promise of a beneficent, all-restoring Last Judgment, there is nothing unusual or incoherent about Benjamin's version; but if it is not to seem ethically facile, it requires more moral pressure than Benjamin exerts on it. In *The Brothers Karamazov,* Ivan asks how anyone can rejoice in humanity's redemption without that joy being undermined by the knowledge of a single tortured child for whom the Messiah came too late. If one traffics in the rhetoric of redemption as much as Benjamin, then at some point it becomes necessary to confront Ivan's question. But Benjamin never quite does so, and that avoidance undermines the seriousness of his theological stance. It is not so much that, in Benjamin's phrase, each age is "endowed with a weak Messianic power,"[13] but rather that his own messianism is endowed with too weak a religious foundation to function as more than a private language, a shorthand for one man's solitary yearnings projected upon history. To invoke the category of the theological after it has been emptied of any specific creed, doctrine, or practice is little more than a verbal gesture at profundity, and there are times when Benjamin's attempt to give his "philosophy of history" a theological dimension comes perilously close to sonorous vacuity. Even at the purely secular level, Benjamin's vocabulary of retrospective redemption is unsatisfying. Horkheimer's sensible objection to the whole idea was simply to remind Benjamin that historical devastation is "irreparable"[14] and that death ends any chance at restitution. Years afterward, reflecting on the Nazi death camps, Primo Levi said that for certain injuries there can be no healing, and that to speak of redemption at all in the context of historical evil is a form of moral blindness: "Once again it must be observed, mournfully, that the injury cannot be healed: it extends through time, and the Furies, in whose existence we are forced to believe, . . . perpetuate the tormentor's work by denying peace to the tormented."[15]

There is no contradiction between Benjamin's messianism and his materialism because he is searching for the same thing in each: a way to bring about a collective, historical consummation comparable in its effect to what Marcel experienced when he tasted the madeleine and found that he had suddenly regained all of his childhood in its incomparable specificity. As with Proust, whom he translated brilliantly into German, it is Benjamin's fidelity to all that has been passed over and discarded that triggers his most moving realizations. Few writers have been more sensitive to how quickly modernity transforms the most up-to-date objects of desire into ridiculous castoffs than Benjamin. As Richard Sieburth has argued, perhaps no one since Baudelaire has written so persuasively about the need for a historian of modernity to become a kind of inspired cultural *chiffonnier*, or ragpicker, combing through the detritus of abandoned fashions.[16] Proust is so crucial a figure for Benjamin not merely because of his theories about time or art, but because Proust's third great theme is idolatry, the worship of false and trivial local gods like social prestige or popularity. Proust's critique of idolatry is also a critique of what the world judges by the criteria of success and power, and it is the antitriumphalism and antipresentism in Proust to which Benjamin is instinctively responsive. Even in "The Life of Students," Benjamin's youthful, self-regarding preciosity gives way to a simpler, more haunting tone when he begins to speak about finding fragments of utopian possibility "deeply embedded in . . . the most endangered, most disparaged and derided" moments. Benjamin was to retain this conviction all his life. His attentiveness to the hopelessly outmoded and obsolete, his resistance to mere "presentism" with its automatic, reflex veneration of whatever has won out in the struggle for success, outshines the often shaky theoretical structures within which he tried to justify his instinctive solicitude. The notorious "garbage heap of history" to which Marxism hoped to consign its vanquished opponents is exactly where Benjamin felt most compelled to linger, and his longing for messianic redemption rings truest when it is spoken on behalf of history's losers without regard to their class allegiances or political views. No sentence in Benjamin, not even the famous description of the storm-hurled "angel of history," is speculatively and ethically richer than his claim in "The Task of the Translator" that "one might . . . speak of an unforgettable life or moment even if all men had forgotten it. If the nature of such a life or moment required that it be unforgotten, that predicate would not imply a falsehood but merely a claim not fulfilled by men, and probably also a reference to a realm in which it is fulfilled: God's remembrance."[17] To realize the potency of Benjamin's formulation, one need think only of the legacy of eastern European Jewry, or of any other community whose culture has been brutally obliterated. To respond to that heritage without guilt or sentimentalizing nostalgia is extraordinarily difficult, but Benjamin is right to insist that there are ways of living in the world whose potential has not been exhausted simply because they were extirpated and whose value should not be judged solely in terms of their longevity and worldly success. He reminds us that there is a moral dimension to remembering even "the most everyday hour" of a vanished existence, and he shows how much painstaking concentration is required to let what was cast aside or defeated be freshly seen in all its singularity. The effort to remain responsive to the unfulfilled possibilities of the past is our only way of disrupting the brutal triumphalism that condemns whatever has perished as deserving its fate because the irresistible logic of history has found it unworthy of continued existence.

Benjamin's father, Emil, had been a partner in one of Berlin's best-known auction houses, and although the two had a difficult and mutually uncomprehending relationship, it was Benjamin's quasi-inherited haute bourgeois predilection for refined connoisseurship that helped foster his most subversively original theories. Benjamin was an inveterate and lifelong collector of everything from old postcards to esoteric books, and he ransacked flea markets looking for too hastily thrown-away treasures in much the same spirit as he went through the great research libraries of Germany and France gathering arcane arguments and precious quotations. His nostalgic affection for the unglamorous objects and stories left behind by history, his often overpowering collector's instinct and inborn melancholy all animate his struggle against what E. P. Thompson has termed "the enormous condescension of posterity"[18] and move him toward a prosaic notion of values. Such a concept—sometimes simply labeled "prosaics"[19]—rejects any notion of historical inevitability. More important, it cherishes the incommensurable value of each human life and contingent moments of lived experiences not for their place in an already determined larger pattern, but as significant in their own right. For prosaics, it is not the moment of crisis that brings out the real value of an individual or of an ethics; ideas, values, and people, according to prosaics, are tested best in the daily, routine actions and habits of ordinary life, not in situations of extraordinary peril. Benjamin's epochal essay on Goethe's *Elective Affinities*,[20] a novel that systematically probes the strength of undramatic domestic values, even against the challenge of overpowering sexual passion, makes clear his sympathetic understanding of prosaics. And only the most acute awareness of the link between the ethical and the narrative dimensions of prosaics could suggest luminous perceptions like Benjamin's praise of the "chronicler who recites events without distinguishing between major and minor ones [and therefore] acts in accordance with the following truth: nothing that has ever happened should be regarded as lost for history."[21]

Incomprehensibly, though, there is scant indication that Benjamin himself was troubled by the contradictions between his antiapocalyptic respect for the abiding value of "everything about history that . . . has been untimely, sorrowful, unsuccessful"[22] and his contemptuous dismissal of time-as-duration. The belief that "nothing that has ever happened should be regarded as lost for history" requires an understanding of time as a succession of content-rich differences, each valid in its own right, rather than as an endless repetition of identically meaningless units suddenly punctuated and redeemed by the thunderclap of the cataclysmically significant crisis. Paradoxically, the gradualism that Benjamin scorns whenever he addresses it directly, and which he regards as the antithesis of his longing for a redemptive transformation, is precisely what animates the only real content he could ever give his utopian images of plenitude. But perhaps it isn't really a question of "contradictions" at all, at least not in the restricted sense of Benjamin's holding incompatible theories and trying to follow divergent intellectual paths. Both of these descriptions certainly apply to Benjamin, and more logically exigent friends such as Scholem and Adorno pressed him repeatedly—and usually in vain—to help them make sense of the palpable contradictions in his theoretical stances. Even at the level of style, rhetoric, and lexical discriminations, Benjamin veered among incompatible tones and registers apparently with as little concern for how awkwardly they sat alongside one another as he was unworried by any formal contradictions in his theories. Thus, for example, his violence-infatuated political rhetoric seems to belong to a different perspective entirely from the patient solicitude with which he discusses finding value in the rejected and jettisoned remnants of an obliterated past. How Benjamin could intersperse passages of unalloyed ethical and imaginative crassness into the mandarin refinement that usually characterizes his writing remains an abiding quandary. It is hard to fathom what frustrated urges prompted a brutish and sexist vignette such as his praise of revolutionary virility in the "Theses on the Philosophy of History": "The historical materialist leaves it to others to be drained by the whore called 'Once upon a time' in historicism's bordello. He remains in control of his powers, man enough to blast open the continuum of history."[23] Benjamin regularly allegorizes sexuality, especially female sexuality, in grating pseudo-aphorisms: "The prostitute represents the consummated will to culture . . . she drives nature from its last sanctuary, sexuality."[24] But it is even more dismaying to hear Benjamin, whose writings on Kafka form one of the few indispensable commentaries on that writer, passively accede to the vileness of Brecht's language about Kafka. On August 5, 1934, a year and a half after Hitler became Germany's chancellor, Benjamin listened to Brecht describe Kafka as "a Jewboy . . . a skinny, unlikable creature, a bubble on the iridescent morass of Prague culture,"[25] without registering any disgust; and later that month Benjamin readily agreed to discuss his own Kafka essay with Brecht in terms of whether or not the essay "advanced Jewish fascism."[26]

Benjamin's at least tacit acquiescence to this kind of viciousness had relatively little to do with any doctrinal political loyalties. It was the ferocity itself that seems to have appealed to him. Throughout his life he was able to respond to the pronunciation of anathemas and execrations without sharing their authors' beliefs. In 1924, he astonished Scholem by taking out a subscription to Charles Maurras's royalist and anti-Semitic paper *Action française*, whose "perspective" he praised as "the only one from which it is possible to view German politics without being stupefied."[27] For the most part, Benjamin preferred his rhetorical violence to be mediated through the voice of a powerful and dogmatic personality like Brecht; but long before he had any interest in Marxist polemics, Benjamin had dreamt of producing an "annihilating criticism"[28] that would obliterate inferior writing with the ruthless "terror" of its judgments. Even as he was composing his essay on *Elective Affinities*, Benjamin boasted to Scholem that his critique would effect "the legally binding condemnation and execution"[29] of Friedrich Gundolf, one of Germany's most influential literary critics whose work Benjamin despised, and Benjamin's correspondence is full of gleefully imagined scenarios of his power to "liquidate" his hapless antagonist. In person, Benjamin was exceptionally diffident and polite, as well as physically awkward, and the rhetoric of terrorism and violence no doubt served as a kind of imaginary redress for the actual vulnerability of an intellectual often frustrated in both his professional ambitions and his personal affairs. Still, such writing was also the unfortunate literary internalization of a climate of savage public abuse and street brawling that marked politics during the Weimar era and helped undermine Germany's short-lived democracy.

In the "Theses on the Philosophy of History," Benjamin insists that "the Messiah comes not only as the redeemer, he comes as the subduer of Antichrist."[30] The messianic is always linked to the destructive in Benjamin, and the allure of messianic violence was not just at the heart of Benjamin's contemptuous impatience with Social Democrats, it also deprived him of any grounds for rejecting the language of violence and imprecation, whether it came from the left via Brecht or from the right via Maurras. What Scholem later called the "catastrophic" tendency of left-wing messianism, the absolutism with which it demands "entirely new aspects of free fulfillment" and disdains anything less than that complete transcendence, is strikingly evident in Benjamin.[31]

But if linking messianic redemption to a final victory over the incarnations of pure evil is a potent theological notion, it has usually had calamitous consequences in the moral and the intellectual realms. Considering that in the twentieth century it was intellectuals, and especially Jewish intellectuals such as Benjamin, who were "liquidated" in countless numbers and places to advance the messianic fantasies of others, there is something almost willfully self-deceiving and self-destructive in his call for a theologically buttressed Marxist revolution.

Curiously, Benjamin's compulsion to act against his own interests, and sometimes even against his chances for survival, has only enhanced the glamour of his posthumous canonization. His life and works have acquired the aura of a legend, and the decisive turning points in his career, from his semideliberate failure to secure the *Habilitation* certification required for teaching at a German university to his suicide after crossing the Pyrenees and reaching Portbou, Spain, in September 1940, have been described so often and with such reverence that they begin to seem like set pieces from an orthodox hagiography. But in any attempt to link Benjamin's life and his writings, the issue of perspective and context is all important, in part because the basic facts are already securely established, and with the exception of a few crucial issues, especially the precise sequence of events in the hours before Benjamin's death from an overdose of morphine, even the most diligent research is unlikely to discover much significant new information. Moreover, although Benjamin's lifelong restlessness and his need to maintain an intricate web of rivalrous erotic and intellectual relationships—what Adorno called Benjamin's "mystery-mongering" pleasure in "keep[ing] his friends apart whenever possible"[32]—provide ample material for an engrossing story, it is "on the page" and in the shifting, often incompatible loyalties of his theoretical allegiances that his most intense experiences took place.

From his cosseted childhood on, Benjamin was extraordinarily ambitious, and yet the choices he made—in his love affairs, in his writing, and even in his lethally tardy response to the Nazi conquest of France—show him courting disaster with the surefooted instinct of a somnambulist. Perhaps he intuited that posterity would be more fascinated by a writer whose life was marked by exemplary failures than by the conventional academic successes of his friends and collaborators such as Scholem, Adorno, or Horkheimer. Most of Benjamin's important projects remained unfinished and unpublished, and yet no one better understood the hold that the fragmentary can have on our imagination. His subject matter and the conduct of his own life were deeply consonant, and the vulnerability he valued in his favorite writers extended to his own self-representation. He repeatedly set up situations that recapitulate, in the personal realm, the same motifs of defeat and loss that propelled his theoretical work. So, for example, when Benjamin opens his diary entry for August 17, 1931, with the melancholy thought that his situation possesses "all the relevance that only hopelessness can give it,"[33] it is hard to imagine that he didn't hear, and perhaps find consolation in, the echo of his own closing lines from the *Elective Affinities* essay: "only for the sake of the hopeless have we been given hope."[34]

But he cared tremendously about his position in the literary world. He was not merely indulging in wish fulfillment when he wrote to Scholem in 1930 that "the goal I had set for myself has not yet been totally realized, but I am finally getting close. The goal is that I be considered the foremost critic of German literature." But rather than talking about any specific personal projects, the letter goes on to offer a fascinating diagnosis of the larger issues at stake: "The problem is that literary criticism is no longer considered a serious genre in Germany and has not been for more than fifty years. If you want to carve out a reputation in the area of criticism, this ultimately means that you must recreate criticism as a genre. Others have made serious progress in doing this, but especially I."[35] Benjamin's ambition, in other words, is to establish literary and cultural criticism as a suitable genre for the creation of a modernist masterpiece. In the previous chapter, I argued that Heidegger consciously intended *Being and Time* as a modernist masterpiece, and that some of its more puzzling characteristics can be understood better by comparing it to contemporary texts like *Ulysses*, the *Duino Elegies*, or Freud's *Standard Edition* than to a conventional philosophical treatise. But there is nothing especially unprecedented about Heidegger's ambition, since the history of philosophy, as much as of art or literature, is rich in ambitious masterpieces whose abiding importance and cultural centrality are readily acknowledged. But literary-cultural criticism is an entirely different matter. It is hard to enumerate more than a handful of such texts that have endured, and most of those are by figures whose fame was secured in the first instance by their achievements as pure philosophers or as authors of poetry and fiction. Even the great literary theoreticians and critics of German Romanticism, like Novalis, Schiller, Schlegel, and Schelling, whom Benjamin implicitly invokes as models and predecessors in his letter to Scholem, all wrote in a multitude of genres including drama, poetry, and novellas, and, like Coleridge in England, the lasting authority of their critical works is directly dependent upon their larger reputation as writers.

But Benjamin never swerved from his project of reestablishing literary-philosophical criticism as a major cultural enterprise. Irrespective of important shifts in idiom or methodology, all of his writing, from before the 1919 Bern University doctoral thesis on "The Concept of Art Criticism in German Romanticism" to the last notes for the unfinished *Arcades Project*, are linked installments of a vast speculative edifice intended to further this ambition. The first step in endowing criticism with the requisite significance is to make it somehow as "difficult" and resistant to a quick and superficial reading as are poetry and modernist fiction. Benjamin opens one of his important essays on Baudelaire with the assertion that "Baudelaire envisaged readers to whom the reading of lyric poetry would present difficulties."[36] For himself, Benjamin envisaged a criticism that would present readers with the same difficulties as the poetry he admired. It was not so much that Benjamin wanted to overthrow the absolute gulf between literature and more ephemeral forms of writing, a gulf that poets like Mallarmé had made central to their conception of art (Mallarmé even spoke of "this precise requirement which commands that if one creates literature one must not use the language of journalism").[37] On the contrary, Benjamin accepts Mallarmé's distinction and then sets about inventing a journalism composed in the language of high literature. In the process, Benjamin virtually creates what is not so much a form as an oxymoron: esoteric journalism, and many of his critical texts are harder to construe and have sparked more controversy than the works they discuss. The success of that project, at least when measured by the number of its imitators in academia today, is indisputable, and no doubt helps explain something of the veneration Benjamin inspires in ambitious literary critics.

Benjamin's whole career shows that he was willing to sacrifice a great deal, and in particular a safe but potentially stultifying university position, to realize his ambition. Legend, some of it initiated by Benjamin himself, has made much of the 1925 rejection by the University of Frankfurt of his *Habilitation* thesis on *The Origin of German Tragic Drama*. But it is clear that Benjamin himself carefully orchestrated an event whose positive outcome he dreaded far more than any failure. The prospect of teaching appalled Benjamin, and years of being supported largely by others, first by his parents and then, until their separation and divorce, by his wife, Dora, made the prospect of a regular job alternately intimidating and a matter of no great importance to him. In the event, though, from the moment of his decisive break with academia and up until the Nazi accession to power, Benjamin's career as a writer and critic flourished as never before. Far from being neglected, as the contemporary myth holds, Benjamin occupied a prominent place in the serious literary journalism of the era. Much of the valuable literary and cultural criticism in Weimar Germany was conducted in the numerous successful journals that sprang up throughout the 1920s, often sponsored by the country's major publishing houses. Momme Brodersen, one of Benjamin's most thorough biographers, reminds us that in these decades Berlin was "the world's greatest newspaper city," with well over two thousand different periodicals available. To one of the most prestigious of these, the *Literarische Welt*, which, at the height of its fame in 1929 had as many as thirty thousand paid readers, Benjamin contributed over one hundred separate articles between October 1925 and February 1933, and the still better established, nationally read *Frankfurter Zeitung* was nearly as hospitable to his writing.[38] Revealingly enough, Benjamin's first publication in both the *Frankfurter Zeitung* and the *Literarische Welt* took place in 1925, coinciding almost exactly with his decision to withdraw his application for a *Habilitation* from the University of Frankfurt. In Germany, the 1920s also marked the beginning of nationwide radio broadcasts, and Benjamin quickly realized the possibilities of the new medium as an important outlet for his work. Between 1929 and 1932, he made more than eighty separate broadcasts for both Frankfurt- and Berlin-based studios. Radio and highbrow journals were equally eager for cultural commentary, and Benjamin was often able to sell the same text with only minor modifications to both. Moreover, his extensive work with this new medium led Benjamin to some of his most probing theoretical inquiries into the influence of the modern technological apparatus on the production, dissemination, and consumption of art.

Like any author, Benjamin confronted rejection and indifference, but compared, for example, to Adorno, Benjamin's early work commanded considerably more attention and respect. Even his immensely difficult book on *The Origin of German Tragic Drama* was favorably reviewed in many of his country's intellectual periodicals as well as in important journals in Hungary, France, Austria, and England. The *Frankfurter Zeitung*, for example, devoted a long article by Siegfried Kracauer to Benjamin's work, and other reviews included a piece in Cambridge University's *Modern Language Review* and Freud's psychoanalytic house organ, *Imago*. And yet it is the image of Benjamin as a marginal, disregarded genius whose radical insights only posterity has been able to appreciate that has become part of our own culture's repertoire of received ideas, fixed so securely that perhaps no factual counterevidence will ever quite dislodge it. Since *we* are that posterity, there is something distastefully self-flattering in the zeal with which Benjamin's legend has been embraced and amplified by his more clamorous admirers. It is our own "enormous condescension" to the enormously variegated and heterogeneous intellectual world that Benjamin inhabited that lets us recycle such thin narratives as the myth that he uniquely embodied European culture's "redemptive" hopes, and it is the scarcely disguised wish to be acclaimed as his successor that prompts literary critics whose circumstances are so utterly different from his to announce their identification with Benjamin's struggles.

Although Benjamin himself had a strong drive toward self-mythologization, he was often also remarkably lucid about his direct collaboration in the catastrophes that befell him. Already in 1932, he admitted to Scholem that "though many—or a sizeable number—of my works have been small-scale victories, they are offset by large-scale defeats."[39] Benjamin was repeatedly drawn to the idea of suicide long before his physical debility and the fear of being turned over to the Nazis caused him to take his own life, and years after her divorce from Benjamin, his ex-wife, Dora, speculated that he had married her primarily to have someone nearby to check his self-destructive impulses. Benjamin characterized himself as a melancholic born "under the sign of Saturn" and found spiritual kinship with writers like Baudelaire, Proust, and Kafka, who understood the seductiveness of despondency. He wrote brilliantly about all three writers, and his descriptions make clear not only the extent of his identification, but also his hope that he, too, might make out of his weaknesses and derelictions the foundation of a great work. He hoped that his loneliness, like Proust's, might be powerful enough "to pull the world down into its vortex with the force of a maelstrom."[40] Nothing in Benjamin's writings seems to me sadder than those moments when he acknowledges the failure of that hope. Referring to his intense labor translating Proust into German, Benjamin wrote, "Unproductive involvement with a writer who so splendidly pursues goals that are similar to my own, at least former, goals occasionally induces something like symptoms of internal poisoning in me."[41] For all his cosmopolitan erudition, there are times when what Benjamin most closely resembles is not one of his literary heroes, but rather the kind of Russian Jew memorably characterized by Isaac Babel as going through life "with spectacles on his nose and autumn in his heart." Nowhere are Benjamin's helplessness and bad luck more apparent than in the unhappy saga of his last-minute flight from Paris in May 1940, first to Lourdes, then to Marseilles, and finally, on September 26, from Banyuls-sur-Mer into Spain. The story has been told numerous times, in biographies, in virtually every introduction to Benjamin's writings, in many of the critical studies devoted to him, and in firsthand accounts by several of the crucial figures involved, notably in *Escape through the Pyrenees*, the gripping memoir by Lisa Fittko, who led the small group that included Benjamin on their illegal trek. The opening of the Spanish archives after Franco's death has also enabled scholars to examine the police and medical files on Benjamin, and recent work on these documents is beginning at last to clarify Benjamin's final hours.

The facile simplifications of the Benjamin legend and the untenability of many of its details unwittingly raise the question of why Benjamin himself never wrote any significant fiction. His contemporaries wondered about this as well, and in 1935 Günther Anders composed a short dialogue, "The Defect," in which Benjamin is described as "lacking something required to write novels . . . that small drop of stupidity and illogicality that a novelist must already have if he is to put it into the mouths of his characters and let them talk realistically."[42] Perhaps. But the explanation seems to me much less interesting than the fact that there was a felt need to provide one in the first place. As so often, Benjamin's own self-description is both harsher and more probing: "I am not interested in people; I am interested only in things."[43] Benjamin sensed that with a temperament such as his, one can write criticism of lasting importance, but not great fiction. No doubt what makes both his messianic longings and his politics so abstract—his inner distance from the ordinary concerns and imaginative life of other people—is exactly what makes him so appealing to academic theoreticians today.

Benjamin has often been accused by friends and critics alike of being unable to commit himself to any one theoretical perspective, emotional attachment, or course of action. But such an accusation misunderstands, I think, the nature of Benjamin's dilemma. Intense commitment posed no threat; it was loss that Benjamin could not accept. Leaving behind anything he had once loved was a source of lasting pain, and since his deepest love was for texts, ideas, and objects, he kept adding to his storehouse of all three like an ardent collector for whom a new acquisition is never meant to supplant earlier ones. The logic of a collection need not be any inner consonance among its components, nor need it be organized according to fixed hierarchic principles; it is sufficient that at one time or another each element had pleased the collector himself. So it is with Benjamin's idiosyncratic appropriations of concepts and rhetorical tropes from mutually antagonistic theoretical positions. "When you're in love, you don't explain, you itemize," is how the poet Frank O'Hara explained the inner affinity between eros and the instinct to generate lists and catalogs. As a collector, Benjamin resisted making hierarchies or weeding anything out, and I doubt that he ever willingly abandoned a single important item from his storehouse of cherished objects and ideas. Benjamin often said that he dreamt of composing a book entirely out of quotations, and the principle of composition-by-collage that such a book would exemplify is central to the whole practice of the modernist masterpiece. (One need think only of a modern verse epic like Ezra Pound's *Cantos* to see how list making and collagist juxtaposition can function as fundamental compositional principles for a major text.) For Benjamin, the citation was an indispensable element of both the work's structure and its intellectual argument. Benjamin was certain that historical fragments, whether literary texts, architectural details, or discarded daily objects, can provide a privileged access to fundamental historical-cultural truths. In this belief, he was only echoing what had actually once been a fairly conventional assumption by nineteenth-century historians like Jacob Burckhardt and which then had been taken up by several noted anthropologists of the generation immediately preceding Benjamin's own. The German anthropologist Leo Frobenius (1873–1938), for example, coined the phrase *Kulturmorphologie*, or cultural morphology, for the conviction that all the essential characteristics of a particular civilization are discernible from a very restricted number of its artifacts. From such a theory Benjamin was able to fashion a linked epistemology and style that gave him two crucial advantages. First, it permitted him to believe that the most fundamental truths, even about as intricate and varied a subject as modern culture, could be grasped (and hence also communicated) by means of individual and even fragmentary "luminous details." Second, it confirmed his intuition that the careful juxtaposition of isolated particulars was not merely the arbitrary gesture of a *littérateur*, but the rigorous application of a coherent theory. Benjamin's juxtapositions and epigrammatic formulations let him present a series of vivid details or images which, when placed together, will "naturally" give rise to a particular argument or interpretation. They will also let him claim that he is only presenting objectively verifiable data for an interpretation that the reader will be all the more ready to accept because of its apparent uncoerciveness. One of the enabling fictions of works like the essays on Baudelaire and the incomplete *Arcades Project* is that Benjamin is merely bringing back into our awareness forgotten or discarded information that had once been quasi-transparent, thereby letting the history of an epoch "present itself" for the edification of the essays' readers. The truth of the narration-through-juxtaposition is guaranteed precisely by the writer's strategic refusal to assume the role of the sole, originating source of argumentation. By allowing the conclusions to arise "inductively" in the reader's mind from the mass of details assembled by the text, Benjamin's writings can claim to be simultaneously both more philosophical and more materialist than standard histories, which sacrifice the local truth of an event for some abstract formula. Yet, paradoxically, specificity indiscriminately applied loses all its specific nature. To connect a mass of sufficiently diverse "particulars," only the most global and abstract links (the evils of the bourgeoisie, the "fallen" state of premessianic history, etc.) can be posited, and the element of history itself, the truth of each "local truth," is lost. The value of juxtapositions to convey a historical and theoretical argument is dependent both on the precise nature of the details brought together and on the mediations, whether these are acknowledged or not, that link the detail to the whole. But, as Adorno repeatedly pointed out in their famous exchanges about the Baudelaire essays, to reflect on their own mediations is what Benjamin's texts absolutely refuse to do. In fact, though, any detailed study of the relationship between an era's cultural production and its political-economic structure is fundamentally uncongenial to Benjamin. He seeks out individual moments and episodes because he is certain that through the "dialectical images" they generate, the whole will be somehow rendered visible. But often, although his images are endlessly suggestive as literary criticism, they do little to offer a convincing interpretation of the specific circumstances and situations from which the items selected originally derive. Most important, what they cannot do is provide a coherent description of the evolving condition of any modern society or its culture. Benjamin's rejection of sequential, gradually unfolding time means that he has no specifically historical way of connecting or differentiating his various "dialectical images."

As so often, Benjamin seems to have realized the problem before any of his critics did, and his fascination with Marxism is part of an ongoing attempt to find a way out of the dilemma. As the limits of *Kulturmorphologie* became increasingly apparent, Benjamin had no choice but to turn to some totalizing explanatory system like Marxism in order to keep writing in his accustomed manner while still claiming a general significance for his local insights and images. What Benjamin hoped Marxism might provide him was a coherent system that was both apocalyptically disruptive of ordinary time and yet able to analyze and classify all the manifestations of any particular moment or epoch. If *Kulturmorphologie* could deduce the basic characteristics of a society from a few artifacts, Benjamin's Marxism promised him much more, since it let him link those same few artifacts to the laws of history as a whole. Because Marxism promises to guarantee the objective truth of the historical conclusions implicit in Benjamin's dialectical images, it permits him in principle to generate an unlimited number of original historical theses by juxtaposition and combination alone (i.e., without analytic proof or step-by-step argumentation). Ultimately, the problem with the introduction of Marxist categories into Benjamin's Jewish-tinged messianism and idealist aesthetics is not their disruptive effect on a series of moving critical speculations and vividly personal insights, nor their "crassness" amid otherwise subtly nuanced perspectives. What is more deeply disconcerting about the class-and-economics-centered arguments that Benjamin actually produces is the way they so transparently recast into a different explanatory mold the same apocalyptic longings and compositional techniques on which his criticism had always relied, thereby exposing similar inadequacies in all of them that might otherwise have been easier to overlook.

Benjamin has frequently been claimed as the inspired predecessor of today's leveling eclecticism, but the impassioned heterogeneity of his approach is very far from the casual irony and unproblematic shuttling among different eras and models that we think of as "postmodernist." The postmodernist catalog is seen from the outset as temporary and easily abandoned. Benjamin's, by contrast, is fiercely cumulative and impossible to discard. And this loyalty to all that has been abandoned as worthless, to everything whose loss has not been acknowledged or registered, is Benjamin's abiding legacy. It is also why it was increasingly difficult for him to complete any of his projects or to save himself when that meant having to leave behind the Bibliothèque Nationale in Paris, where he had been free to spend his days seeking out long-forgotten treasures. Benjamin's often remarked upon many-sidedness, his curiosity and love of exploring new domains and relationships, makes him not unlike a modern, intellectualized version of what Homer calls Odysseus: *polytropos,* "a man of many turnings." But Odysseus's many-mindedness helped him survive and return home, whereas Benjamin's doomed him physically and sabotaged most of his cherished intellectual projects. His simultaneous fidelity to a few governing impulses and desires, combined with an inability to commit himself to a single course of action, a person, a belief, or even an intellectual trajectory, is both his best and worst quality. Indeed, throughout his life as well as writings, his best and his most self-limiting tendencies were hopelessly intertwined. Of all the critical comments on Proust made by other writers, Benjamin most admired Jacques Rivière's remark that "Marcel Proust died of the same inexperience of the world which permitted him to write his works."[44] Benjamin's identification with such a description is obvious, but his own case is still more paradoxical. It is true that the unworldliness and the loyalty to his obsessions that undermined his chances to reach a safe refuge after the fall of France simultaneously enabled his finest writing; but these same traits also guaranteed that much of that writing would never be developed beyond disparate notations of luminous details.

Benjamin's true self-portrait exists more fully in his comments on the writers he most valued than in his explicitly autobiographical works like *One-Way Street,* his memoir of the Berlin of his childhood and adolescence. In 1938, he closed a lengthy letter to Gershom Scholem about Kafka with a summary that reads uncannily—and in all likelihood quite intentionally—like a model for his own epitaph:

To do justice to the figure of Kafka . . . one must never lose sight of one thing: it is the figure of a failure. The circumstances of this failure are manifold. One is tempted to say: once he was certain of eventual failure, everything worked out for him *en route* as in a dream. There is nothing more memorable than the fervor with which Kafka emphasized his failure.[45]

Benjamin's words are painfully precise about himself, if not necessarily about Kafka. The longing for redemption and the critique of culture were never integrated into the great modernist masterpiece about which Benjamin dreamed for more than a decade. Yet his failure continues to fascinate more than many of the "successes" of his contemporaries—and Benjamin, the great connoisseur of defeats and lost causes, would have understood that fascination better than anyone.

Paul Celan
Radiance That Will Not Comfort

"I wanted most of all . . . to tell you—with what words, with what silence?—
that you must not believe words like yours can remain unheard." *Mit welchen Worten,
welchem Schweigen?*[1] The delicacy of Celan's question to Nelly Sachs, his fellow poet
and Shoah-haunted exile, and the tact with which he hesitates between stillness
and speech, even as he offers her the solace of both, is characteristic of the tension
at the heart of his own utterances as a poet. But here, in this letter of January
1958, by speaking more as a bringer of comfort than as another bruised Holocaust
survivor or companion in inner devastation, Celan can allow his phrase to resonate
with an equipoise that embraces both impulses; his words reach as much toward
muteness as toward articulation, the two coexisting without shattering the larger
frame of the care-filled dialogue that contains them.

And yet, at the level of syntax, the interjection, like many of Celan's more
celebrated formulations, attests to an irreparable inner fissure. "With what words,
with what silence?": the phrase sharply divides in half, with the second element
almost, but never entirely, undoing the first. There is all the difference in the world
between being silent and being silenced, but for a European Jew who managed to
survive the genocidal onslaught of Nazism, the two categories, a freely chosen,
responsive silence and the empty muteness of extermination, will remain eerily
linked in an intractable and purely destructive psychic bond.

The exploration of silence (and of its corollary, absence) as an aesthetic
resource in its own right has been one of modernism's central projects, at least
since Mallarmé's *Un Coup de Dés* tried to make the circumambient blankness of the
page as much a part of the poem's rhythm as the pacing and length of its actual
words. Think of Cézanne's watercolors, where the whiteness of the untreated
paper is crucial to defining the composition's different elements and demarcating
their spatial proportions, or the emotion-laden intervals between the separate
notes in Webern's chamber music, and it will be clear that in the first half of

the twentieth century each of the arts was enriched by a complex repertory of techniques intended to marshal both the formal and the psychological power of silence. But for a Jew writing in the aftermath of the Shoah, the choice of silence as a way to register now forever inaudible articulations, the felt pressure of bodies and forms that no longer exist, has an entirely different force, all the more so if that Jewish writer is also a hyperconscious inheritor of the whole modernist tradition with all its ambition and restless self-interrogation.

I know of no other figure of whom such a description is truer than Paul Celan (1920–70), the adopted name of Paul Pessach Antschel, whose collected works constitute the one indispensable body of verse written in German since the death of Rilke in 1926.[2] Yet if Celan's centrality among the greatest poets of the century has become virtually axiomatic, at least for the German-speaking world, the radical solitude of his situation and his achievement has also kept him a figure apart. He is a writer exemplary of, but also eccentric to, a language whose integrity his work did so much to restore in the aftermath of its wholesale degradation during the Third Reich.

Even the most fragmentary details of Celan's personal existence, as they are slowly emerging from the shelter of his intensely guarded privacy, show the immense psychic cost of his burden as a Jewish artist who was compelled, by his own imperious gifts, to compose his works in the same language as the murderers of his parents, his community, and his world. In a sense, Celan's works are the final, wrenching enactment of the triple impossibility Kafka had already outlined in a famous letter to Max Brod in June 1921 about the dilemma facing Jewish writers composing in German:

> [T]he product of their despair could not be German literature, though outwardly it seemed to be so. They existed among three impossibilities . . . These are: The impossibility of not writing, the impossibility of writing in German, the impossibility of writing differently. One might also add a fourth impossibility, the impossibility of writing (since the despair could not be assuaged by writing, was hostile to both life and writing; writing is only an expedient, as for someone who is writing his will shortly before he hangs himself—an expedient that may well last a whole life).[3]

After the Shoah, though, what were still in part personal psychological burdens for Kafka become ferociously historical and all-encompassing. For Celan, the mother tongue stands in unbearable intimacy with the murderers' tongue, the cadences of his mother's favorite songs and fairy tales recapitulated in the rhetoric that conceived, organized, and then implemented the Final Solution. The words of the lullabies on which he was raised could never be entirely dissociated from what he later called "the thousand darknesses of deathbringing speech."[4] But the astonishing fact remains that no matter how lacerating the effort, Celan made out of that terrible contradiction the fulcrum of his greatest poems. Where other survivors found the very sound of German unendurable and either lapsed into silence or, like Dan Pagis, left Europe altogether for Israel and began to write in Hebrew, Celan answered the repeated questions addressed to him about his decision to continue writing in German by insisting that "only in one's mother tongue can one express one's own truth; in a foreign language the poet lies."[5]

Born a Romanian citizen, and then in 1955 becoming a naturalized French one, Celan scarcely ever inhabited a country whose official language was German. Yet he never stopped composing German poems. He did so in the Czernowitz ghetto into which he and the other Jews of his hometown were herded in 1941, and he continued writing in German, often in rhythms and imagery derived from old German ballads as well as from Hölderlin, Rilke, and Trakl, while enduring the brutish regime of the forced labor camps in Falticeni and Buzau (Romania), where he was held from July 1942 until early 1944. And it was in a German poem that he first tried to frame a response to the news of his parents' death. As Celan explained in a much-quoted self-definition he offered to a friend in 1948, "there is nothing in the world for which a poet will give up writing, not even when he is a Jew and the language of his poems is German."[6] But underneath the seeming assurance of this sentence lies all the compacted anxiety with which Celan loaded the crucial word "nothing." It was into "nothing in the world," after all, that the Germans sought to reduce Jewish existence; and in the haunting phrase from "Death Fugue," Celan's best-known poem, it was the nothingness of "a grave in the air"[7] that awaited the Jews of the ghettos and death camps. And it was into a barren nothingness, lacking even a sure location or a fixed date, that Celan's own mother and father vanished forever. (The best historical assumption, which cannot be definitely confirmed, is that Leo Antschel, Celan's father, was deported to the Michailowka camp in the Ukraine, where he died from typhus in the fall of 1942, and that the poet's mother, Friederike, was shot a few months later because she was no longer useful as a slave laborer.)

In "Psalm," which remains one of the very few poems in any language to confront directly the annihilation of European Jewry without seeming presumptuous, *ein Nichts*, "a nothing," becomes the root term of a whole series of undoings that amount to a radical subversion of the millennial tradition of religious songs of worship or lamentation, as well as of the German metaphysical rhetoric that culminated in Heidegger's writings:

Ein Nichts
waren wir, sind wir, werden
wir bleiben blühend:
die Nichts—, die
Niemandsrose.
       "Psalm"

> A nothing
> we were, are, shall
> remain, flowering:
> the nothing—, the
> no one's rose.
>
> "Psalm"[8]

For Heidegger, *das Nichts* is the very ground against and within which *Dasein* emerges and from which it derives its significance. Hence his general, hypostatizing term, *"the* Nothing[ness]." For Celan, though, and the change is both deliberate and decisive, European Jewry has been reduced only to *"a* nothing," without Heideggerian metaphysical attributes or redemptive significance. Chosen flowers of an absent God ("Blessèd are thou, No One") who was unable to save His people from being turned into the airy vacancy of ashes and wind, Celan's voices have made out of the nothingness of their futile despair an indictment (which, like all verse "complaints," also carries the suggestion of a song of thwarted or blocked love) against a Creator who has lost the power to bring forth new life out of so much suffering:

> Niemand knetet uns wieder aus Erde und Lehm,
> niemand bespricht unsern Staub.
> Niemand.
>
> "Psalm"

> No one moulds us again out of earth and clay,
> no one conjures our dust.
> No one.
>
> "Psalm"[9]

In his book *Fadensonnen*, or *Threadsuns*, which appeared in 1968, Celan described his poetics as *die Spur eines Bisses im Nirgends*, "the trace of a bite in the Nowhere," or, less literally, "the trace of a bite-mark onto/into Nothingness,"[10] and much of his writing can be seen as an unraveling of the implications of King Lear's "Nothing will come of nothing" for our age of industrialized mass murder. So the "nothing in the world for which a poet will give up writing," which Celan invoked almost at the outset of his career, is not only his declaration of a literary calling, but a figure for all the piled-up absences that will compel both his most emotionally charged utterances and the silence of suicide that, at age forty-nine, he ultimately chose.

We still know very little about Celan's last weeks, but the ever increasing extremity of his desolation was unmistakable even before he took his own life in Paris around April 20, 1970. (George Steiner has pointed out how uncanny Celan's timing was, since April 20 was also Hitler's birthday and as such was celebrated as one of the Third Reich's principal holidays.) One of Celan's poems speaks of a "radiance that will not comfort,"[11] and his writing continually questions the value of its own moments of illumination because of their impotence in the face of so much loss. Yet there is no truth in the banal image of Celan as an unrecognized genius whose work was too challenging to be appreciated by his contemporaries. Quite the contrary. What is surprising is how early Celan found an attentive audience, how quickly his reputation as a major writer was secured.

When he arrived in Vienna in December 1947, after an illegal and arduous escape from Bucharest, he brought with him a letter of introduction from Alfred Margul-Sperber, the noted Jewish Bukovina poet, who described Celan as "the most original and unmistakable of the recent German generation . . . [Celan's poetry is] the only lyric counterpart to Kafka's work."[12] Celan was soon invited to give readings both in public and on Austrian radio; his work appeared in an important avant-garde magazine, and in 1948, after he had already left for Paris, his first book, *Der Sand aus den Urnen (The Sand from the Urns),* was released by a Viennese publisher. Although the misprints and the cheap postwar paper and binding made Celan withdraw the volume, his own letters confirm that, with only some exaggeration, he felt himself on the way to being regarded as "the greatest poet in Austria and . . . in Germany as well."[13] Celan also made a number of important friends in Austria, including the writer Ingeborg Bachmann (1926–73), whose university dissertation on Heidegger and deep concern for the relationship of his thought to Nazism helped give Celan at least a temporary sense of artistic kinship in an environment in which he quickly began to feel ill at ease. In 1952, when a Stuttgart publisher brought out *Mohn und Gedächtnis (Poppy and Remembrance),* a greatly expanded collection which retained the best poems from *The Sand from the Urns,* Celan immediately became one of the most widely discussed poets in the country. The book was reviewed in many of the leading German newspapers, including the *Frankfurter Allgemeine Zeitung* and *Die Zeit,* and its central poem, "Todesfuge," or "Death Fugue," almost overnight became the country's single most commented upon, reprinted, and officially canonized poem about the Shoah. The poem's unprecedented and almost instantaneous reception helped fuel Celan's later suspicion that it was being misused to validate an emptily sentimental and offensively aestheticized reconciliation between Germans and Jews.

But neither its familiarity nor the sometimes dubious reasons for its initial success should blind one to how astonishing a work "Death Fugue" really is. From the opening lines, the poem's force and originality are palpable:

Schwarze Milch der Frühe wir trinken sie abends
　wir trinken sie mittags und morgens wir trinken sie nachts
　wir trinken und trinken

wir schaufeln ein Grab in den Lüften da liegt man nicht eng
Ein Mann wohnt im Haus der spielt mit den Schlangen der
     schreibt
der schreibt wenn es dunkelt nach Deutschland dein goldenes Haar
     Margarete
er schreibt es und tritt vor das Haus und es blitzen die Sterne er
     pfeift seine Rüden herbei
er pfeift seine Juden hervor läßt schaufeln ein Grab in der Erde
er befiehlt uns spielt auf nun zum Tanz

                                                    "Todesfuge"

Black milk of daybreak we drink it at evening
we drink it at midday and morning we drink it at night
we drink and we drink
we shovel a grave in the air there you won't lie too cramped
A man lives in the house he plays with his vipers he writes
he writes when it grows dark to Deutschland your golden hair
     Margareta
he writes it and steps out of doors and the stars are all sparkling
     he whistles his hounds to come close
he whistles his Jews into rows has them shovel a grave in the ground
he commands us play up for the dance

                                        "Death Fugue"[14]

    Perhaps the most astonishing feature of this poem, even more than its hypnotic rhythms and images, is the daring with which it voices the experience of the death factories in the first person plural and in the present tense. The "we" who speak the words of the poem are Jewish prisoners in one of the extermination camps; and by using the first person and permitting himself this act of imaginative ventriloquism, Celan directly violates one of the central moral-aesthetic prohibitions of our time. "Death Fugue" demonstrates that poetry *can* imagine the unimaginable, create a language for what is unsayable, and give memorable shape to catastrophic experiences that are not autobiographically grounded. The real "scandal" of "Death Fugue" is its transgression of the sole almost universally agreed-upon taboo arising out of the Shoah: the injunction against anyone except a survivor presuming to represent directly the thoughts and feelings of prisoners in a death camp. "Death Fugue" is testimony through imagination, and the interdiction against "fictional testimony" is, if anything, even greater today than when the poem was originally published.[15] Indeed, so strong is our age's suspicion of the imagination, and so unshakable its faith that only biographical testimony can ring true, that not only were numerous early critics convinced Celan must himself be a concentration camp survivor, but the same misinformation continued to be propagated long after he became famous and is still regularly recycled today, three decades after his death. In an essay introducing a 1987–88 traveling exhibition of Anselm Kiefer's paintings, for example, Mark Rosenthal, one of the curators of twentieth-century art at the Guggenheim Museum, writes, "No theme has ever occupied Kiefer so deeply as Margarete and Shulamite. This subject is founded on an excruciatingly painful poem entitled 'Death Fugue' (Todesfuge) by Paul Celan, written in a concentration camp in 1945 and published in 1952."[16] In its own lengthy piece on Kiefer, the *New York Times Magazine* gave still wider circulation to the same error. They reproduced Kiefer's 1981 painting, "Your golden hair, Margarethe," and described it as follows: "the painting was inspired by Paul Celan's 'Death Fugue,' a poem he wrote in a concentration camp."[17] Nor are strictly literary sources always more reliable. In the introduction to her successful 1995 anthology *Holocaust Poetry*, Hilda Schiff mentions " 'Death Fugue' by Paul Celan, himself a former camp inmate," and in the "Biographical Details" at the volume's end, she not only errs about where Celan's parents actually perished but elides any difference between labor and extermination camps: "In 1942 Celan saw his parents deported to Auschwitz. He himself survived in other camps, but never recovered and in 1970 committed suicide. (Compare Primo Levi and Tadeusz Borowski.)"[18] More revelatory, still, though, is how Celan himself seemed to have begun to doubt the moral legitimacy of speaking in the voice of a "we" whose fate he had not directly undergone. Certainly his later writing was much more cautious in the way it permitted itself such liberties, and some of his subsequent dissatisfaction with "Death Fugue" may have been due not only to its facile appropriation by German educators and politicians, but also to its fluency in engaging a subject that he came to feel ought to force from him more halting and hesitant tones. Every line of "Death Fugue" shows the dazzling technical and imaginative mastery of its author, and there *is* something unsettling about such sovereign control—and the unavoidable sense of textual delight that always accompanies demonstrations of such artistic power—when the poem's subject is the utter helplessness of the Shoah's victims. "Death Fugue" accomplished something that perhaps Celan ultimately thought morally inadmissible: it is a deliberate, triumphantly successful modernist masterpiece about the genocide of European Jewry, and as such it could not survive as the foundation for a new postwar aesthetic. Although his own situation and subject give the problem an incomparably sharper edge, Celan's anxiety about the ethical legitimacy of what he had accomplished in these poems takes up a question that already haunted Coleridge in his *Notebooks*: does the fact that poetry "excites us to artificial feelings" necessarily mean that it "makes us callous to real ones"?[19] The fundamental, grounding faith of the modernist masterpiece, the belief that great art can somehow redeem even the most damaged and damaging human experience, could not survive the brute truth of the Shoah, and "Death Fugue" may be the last luminous example of a modernist masterpiece in all its undiminished ambition.

Soon after these first poems were published, Celan systematically began to strip himself of the medievalism and Rilkean echoes that still dominated much of *Poppy and Remembrance*. Derivative and overly luxurious lines like the surrealist-influenced "Green as mould is the house of oblivion. / Before each of the blowing gates your beheaded minstrel turns blue" from "The Sand from the Urns,"[20] or "we love each other like poppy and recollection, / we sleep like wine in the conches, / like the sea in the moon's blood ray" from "Corona,"[21] gave way to a more austere language. In 1955 Celan's next book, *Von Schwelle zu Schwelle (From Threshold to Threshold)*, raised the issue of the poet's responsibility to his subject matter with unforgiving directness:

> Welchen der Steine du hebst—
> du entblößt,
> die des Schutzes der Steine bedürfen . . .
> Welches der Worte du sprichst—
> du dankst
> dem Verderben.
>   "Welchen der Steine du hebst"

> Whichever stone you lift—
> you lay bare
> those who need the protection of stones . . .
> Whichever word you speak—
> you owe
> to destruction.
>   "Whichever Stone You Lift"[22]

The image of martyred bodies hidden beneath stones carries unmistakable echoes of Christ's entombment after Calvary, and Celan's daring appropriation of one of the central iconographic moments in the crucifixion story for the fate of the Jews is characteristic of the freedom with which he draws upon the entire European cultural tradition throughout his writing. Though Jewish themes and motifs are foundational, they are far from all-determining, and Celan's allusive range is completely uncircumscribed by the self-censorship demanded by zealots of identity politics. Christian topoi are as important an imaginative resource for Celan as traditional Jewish ones, and often the two are simultaneously invoked, not in a spirit of reconciliation, but rather to emphasize the dreadful historical asymmetry between the fate of two peoples. Here, for example, the radical inversion of the Christian story helps bring out the bitterness of the fate of Europe's Jews. The boulder that sealed off Christ's sepulchre was rolled away by an angel to reveal the miracle of an empty grave and a resurrected savior; but for the nameless ones beneath these stones there is no resurrection, only a need for shelter that extends beyond the limits of physical life itself because the injury they sustained was so deep. But even poems like "Whichever Stone You Lift," although stripped of the high rhetoric and historical ventriloquism of "Death Fugue," are, for Celan, still almost too grammatically and syntactically untroubled and too composed in their figuration of rupture. A decisive and permanent shift in Celan's writing away from what still left him dissatisfied with the language and technique he had developed through his first three books is clearly evident in the 1959 collection *Sprachgitter* (*Speech-Grille*). The darkness of the Shoah is no longer only a thematic obsession; it seems to have penetrated the poet's very language, compelling him toward a new kind of speech: an articulate reticence in which suffering is recognizable more by its speechlessness than by its capacity to cry out. So in "Tenebrae," when Celan again dares to assume the voice of those who went "wind-skewed" into the "pit and crater" of death (*windschief*, the German term, is one of the many brilliant and untranslatable neologisms Celan invented in this volume), he does so without the careful "stage-setting" of "Death Fugue." Although the imagery of bodies twisted in the agony of the gas chambers is unmistakable, there is no more mention of a Nazi camp commander, like the "Master from Germany" at whose behest the "Death Fugue" was performed. In its place, there remains only the deeper argument with a God who has been damaged as deeply as His people by the genocide:

> Nah sind wir, Herr,
> nahe und greifbar.
>
> Gegriffen schon, Herr,
> ineinander verkrallt, als wär
> der Leib eines jeden von uns
> dein Leib, Herr.
>
> Bete, Herr,
> bete zu uns,
> wir sind nah.
>
> Windschief gingen wir hin,
> gingen wir hin, uns zu bücken
> nach Mulde und Maar.
> "Tenebrae"
>
> We are near, Lord,
> near and at hand.
>
> Handled already, Lord,
> clawed and clawing as though

the body of each of us were
Your body, Lord.

Pray, Lord,
pray to us,
we are near.

Wind-awry we went there,
went there to bend
over hollow and ditch.
                    "Tenebrae"[23]

"Tenebrae" was partially inspired by François Couperin's (1668–1733) cantata *Leçons de Ténèbres*, a setting of the Lamentations of Jeremiah, and throughout the poem, Celan maintains an immensely daring interlacing of Jewish and Christian themes. John Felstiner, Celan's most reliable biographer, tells us that in the first draft of the poem, Celan initially kept Couperin's French title, but then changed his mind and chose "Tenebrae" because "he preferred the Latin's priestly character."[24] "Tenebrae" is also dense with direct echoes of and challenges to Hölderlin's great poem "Patmos," a text that was central to Heidegger's reading of Hölderlin. Celan's title, "Tenebrae" (shadows, or darkness), is from the Catholic liturgy during Holy Week, when the extinguishing of the candles, one by one, is symbolic of the darkness that spread over the earth at the moment of Christ's death on the cross: *A sexta autem hora tenebrae facta sunt super universam terram usque ad horam nonam* (Now from the sixth hour there was darkness over all the land unto the ninth hour [Matt. 27:45]). In a condensed form, even Celan's dazzling invention of *windschief*, or "wind-awry" ("wind-skewed" in Felstiner's more powerful rendering), for a people who have been turned into smoke and ashes enacts the entire Jewish-Christian tension of the poem. As Margarita Yanson, a medievalist graduate student at Berkeley, showed me, Celan's coinage clearly echoes Gottfried von Strassburg's daring comparison of Christ to a windblown sleeve in his early thirteenth-century version of *Tristan*:

> dâ wart wol g'offenbaeret,
> und al der werlt bewaeret,
> daz der vil tugenthafte Crist
> *wintschaffen* alse ein ermel ist

> Thus it was manifest
> and confirmed to all the world
> that Christ in His great virtue
> is pliant as a windblown sleeve.[25]

Celan's transformation of Gottfried's *wintschaffen* into *windschief* is crucial to "Tene-brae" since it marks the failure of the divine mercy that was so richly manifest in the medieval text. In *Tristan*, Christ intervenes to ensure Isolde's successful passing of a trial by hot iron, thereby establishing her innocence from the charge of adultery before the courtiers and bishops of England, even though she clearly betrayed her husband, King Mark. In Gottfried's poem, the judgment of Christ is not bound by the norms of the human institutions of justice. His judgment is based on the inward virtue of love between Tristan and Isolde, rather than on their outward transgressions. Celan's poem, too, is deeply concerned with the question of judgment and righteousness, and it refers to a dreadful ordeal by fire as well, but this time there was no mercy or justice even though the windblown people of his poem, unlike Isolde, were entirely guiltless. The catastrophic failure of divine justice renders God himself *unjust* in Celan's poem, and hence it is God who is now in need of forgiveness from those who, being themselves obliterated, are no longer there to absolve him. The community of Christian worshipers at mass on Easter Sunday celebrate a rebirth after suffering, a lifting of the darkness; the dead Jews of the Shoah have nothing left to celebrate, no resurrection for which to hope. For the survivors, Easter itself is largely a reminder of a season associated with pogroms and fear, and the "lessons of the shadows" that ring so evocatively inside a church are here contrasted with the very different "lesson" inflicted on the inhabitants of the ghettos and camps. Celan uses the central, redemptive tropes of the Christian liturgical imagination in order to intensify the bitterness of the historical victims of that imagination. In doing so he has created a doubled "we," Christian and Jew using the same words to say entirely different— indeed, antithetical—things. This is, perhaps, the only form of a "German-Jewish dialogue" still imaginable for Celan. But beyond its immediate effectiveness in "Tenebrae," this technique of layered, contradictory echoes enables Celan to retain the first-person plural voice of "Death Fugue" without leaving himself open to the charge of illicit ventriloquism. "Tenebrae" is actually even bolder than "Death Fugue" in the way it speaks for the victims of the Shoah. It directly takes up the collective voice of all those murdered during the Shoah, whether in death camps, ghettos, or killing fields, and speaks in their voice without needing to locate itself in any one specifically identifiable setting. The text's own resistance to straightforward narrative continuity, its fragmentary, broken utterances, and its avoidance of the careful dramatization of "Death Fugue," with the risk of a totalizing rhetoric implicit in such a precise dramatization, makes its use of the first person seem less like a gesture of poetic presumption than like a haunting by disparate voices whose tones exceed the poet's capacity to master them and give them a stable identity. The simultaneous abstraction and specificity of the poem's language as a whole extends to the "we" who are its speakers, and in that physically vivid but eerily abstract—because obliterated—collective voice, Celan found a way to avoid some of the artistic self-display inherent in a modernist masterpiece like "Death Fugue."

It is a critical commonplace that poems like "Tenebrae" and "Engführung" ("Stretto"), the concluding poem of *Speech-Grille*, are reworkings of "Death Fugue"'s themes, only with a different poetics. But what is at issue is far more than a change in style. It is a radical transformation of the whole relationship between speech and silence in the face of annihilation and thus a revocation of the foundational premises of the modernist lyric from Mallarmé until early Celan himself. In that high modernist tradition, silence had always functioned as the guardian of the poem's separate and autonomous purity. For Mallarmé, the whiteness of the page is there "to authenticate the silence" (*authentiquer le silence*) that endows the language of poetry with its significance.[26] Celan and Mallarmé are among the two most formally rigorous and syntactically complex poets in their respective languages, and each of them placed silence and absence at the center of his poetics. But silence speaks differently after the genocide. For Mallarmé, it is language itself that provides the dialogic situation that makes silence significant; for Celan, it is the human, especially the Jewish and familial community that was also required to add the dimension of meaning to silence and nothingness, and after the destruction of that community, silence can no longer be fully "authenticated." What is left when language ruptures in this way are broken shards of speech, and Celan's lines sometimes read like fragments that have survived from what had once been a more complete text:

> Asche.
> Asche, Asche.
> Nacht.
> Nacht-und-Nacht. —Zum
> Aug geh, zum feuchten.
> . . . .
>
> Verbracht
> ins Gelände
> mit
> der untrüglichen
> Spur:
>
> Gras.
> Gras,
> auseinandergeschrieben.
>   "Engführung"

Ashes.
Ashes, ashes.
Night.
Night-and-Night. —Find
that eye, the moist one.

Taken off
to the terrain
with
the unerring
trace:

Grass.
Grass,
written asunder.
"Stretto"²⁷

What Celan accomplishes in these poems is almost unprecedented in postwar literature. He creates a powerful, immediately recognizable lyric voice that carries him through entire poetic sequences while carefully avoiding grounding that voice in a set of continuous personal characteristics. Many of the poems read like aborted apostrophes, frustrated gestures attempting to address a listener who is silent, indifferent, or simply no longer there. Each rebuff seems to push Celan's language further into its own resources, and in succeeding volumes, his poetry becomes even more concentrated, his effects more dependent upon releasing the energy of a single word, or even a single syllable and the silence surrounding it, rather than on the long lines, the regular iambic and dactylic meters, and the rich rhymes of the first book. The intense pressure on each element of the poem— diction, syntax, rhythm—sometimes leads to a series of unprecedented (and largely untranslatable) word formations, such as the uncannily precise *auseinandergeschrieben* (written asunder) for the paradox of the preservation and dispersal of Jewish traces in both the grass of the concentration camps and on the pages of the poem; *Rauchseele* (smoke-soul) for those who were incinerated in the Nazi crematoria as well as for the transience and fragility of what makes us human in the first place; or *Meingedicht* (my perjury-poem) for Celan's bitter rejection of what he had come to think of as the gaudiness of his own earlier verse. At other times, the same pressure compels the terrible clarity of lines like these:

Niemand
zeugt für den
Zeugen.
"Aschenglorie"

Nobody
bears witness for the
witness.
                    "Ashglory"[28]

And yet neither Celan's discarding of the poetic techniques that had established his
reputation nor the turbulence of his private life led to any diminution in the rapidity
or the quantity with which he produced new writing. Brilliant translations into
German of poets like Mandelstam, Blok, Yesenin, Valéry, Michaux, Shakespeare,
and Ungaretti appeared at regular intervals, and starting in 1959, Celan was
employed in Paris as a teacher of German at the École Normale Supérieure.
His letters often speak of feeling sterile and blocked, but collections such as *Die
Niemandsrose* (*The No-One's Rose*) in 1963, *Atemwende* (*Breathturn*) in 1967, *Fadensonnen*
(*Threadsuns*) in 1968, and the posthumously published *Lichtzwang* (*Light-Compulsion*
or *Force of Light*) in 1970, *Schneepart* (*Snow-Part*) in 1971, and *Zeitgehöft* (*Farmstead
of Time*) in 1976 actually suggest a remarkable intensification in the urgency with
which Celan kept on composing.

    Despite Celan's refusal to live in Germany, the appearance there of each of
his books was regarded as an important cultural event, and between 1956 and
1964 he was awarded the country's four major literary prizes. Celan used one of
these occasions, the award of the Georg Büchner Prize in Darmstadt in 1960, to
produce "The Meridian," a deeply searching statement about the nature of modern
poetry. Indeed, although by comparison to the major high modernist poets like
T. S. Eliot or Ezra Pound, Celan published very little criticism or prose "defenses"
of his own poetics, the few pieces he did write, especially "The Meridian" and
"Conversation in the Mountains," have become touchstones of postwar theorizing
about the condition of poetry "after Auschwitz." In its rhetorical density and
charged indirection, Celan's prose is scarcely distinguishable from his verse, and
when he insists in "The Meridian" that the poem must speak "on behalf of the
other . . . perhaps of an altogether other," it is poetry's obligation to bear witness
for the now speechless witnesses that we hear affirmed. As long as what Celan
calls poetry's "desperate conversation" can be sustained, as long, that is, as its
"strong tendency towards silence"[29] and its responsibility toward those who were
consigned to ashes do not annul one another, some kind of lyric voice might still
be able to authenticate its utterances. But the nature of that lyric "I" has become
alarmingly fragile and hard to locate in either a place or a time. If all the true
addressees of the lyric voice are now themselves outside time, if, that is, they
have been violently excised from the world, then in order to address them, it
is necessary to posit a voice which is itself outside of time and hence not part
of any living continuum. And yet all of Celan's writing resists the Mallarméan
urge to make language itself poetry's only concern. For all its intricacy, nothing

could be further from Celan's poetics than a celebration of art's self-sufficiency. On the contrary, Celan insists that "the poem intends an other, needs this other" and is forever "on the way" to the other.[30] As Krzysztof Ziarek aptly puts it, for Celan, "the other does not appear merely as a theme, an image or a series of images in the poem, but, conversely, all aspects of the poem, its imagery, meaning, rhythm, point toward the other."[31] Celan's language and syntax are almost literally fractured between the bleakness of an imposed solitude and the ceaselessly renewed attempt to find an answering voice, and the resulting strain helps account for the dislocations and abrupt changes in register and tone of his poetry. Since Celan's texts seem at once so oblique and yet so unmistakably rooted in personal anguish, and since his fate seems both so isolated and yet so emblematic, it is difficult not to be fascinated by his life and grateful for any elucidations that biography can offer. And I think this holds true even if we share Celan's distaste for the chatter of literary biography that merely intrudes between the reader and the poem. Even relatively brief documents, such as Celan's correspondence with Nelly Sachs or the still untranslated ones with Margul-Sperber, Petre Solomon, and Franz Wurm, can be more useful than many of the labored theoretical exegeses that have tried to appropriate Celan for various transient academic projects. Most of all, though, we need an adequately annotated critical edition of the poems themselves to replace the almost shockingly unhelpful five-volume *Collected Works* of 1983.

An annotated edition is especially important because the range of Celan's allusions and the provenance of many of his linguistic coinings are so different from those of any other important twentieth-century German-language writer. The crucial impact on Celan of the Hebrew Bible, and, via Gershom Sholem and Martin Buber, of Kabbalistic and Hassidic lore, has long been recognized, but recent research, buttressed by information from the poet's voluminous and still largely unpublished notebooks, greatly extends our sense of how central these sources are. Moreover, it is not only Hebrew and Yiddish that nourish the radical polyphony of Celan's language. Romanian, Russian, and French are also imaginatively and lexically vital to Celan's verbal inventiveness, and both English and Italian, although less pivotal, are nonetheless tangible presences in many of his formulations. Evaluating the nature of these diverse strains in Celan is a process that we are only beginning to undertake with a sufficiently sharp sense of what is at stake. For example, along with his readings in Scholem and Buber, it is clear that Celan also had a lifelong interest in Jakob Böhme (1575–1624), who found a mystical etymology at the core of the German language itself. Celan's fascination with the hidden sense of words owes as much to Böhme as to Kabbalah, and my own sense is that Celan was attracted precisely to those aspects of Jewish knowledge that strengthened and gave new inflections to passions he had already developed from other sources. What has become increasingly clear in the three decades since

Celan's death, though, is how partial and restricting it is to think of him, in any normative sense, as a *German* poet at all.

I mean this quite straightforwardly. When Paul Antschel was born on November 23, 1920, in Czernowitz, the town had only been part of Romania for two years. Before 1918, Czernowitz, called "little Vienna" by its large and culturally flourishing Jewish population, was the capital of Bukovina, the easternmost crown land of the Habsburg monarchy. Celan occasionally called himself a "posthumously born *Kakanier*,"[32] and his use of Robert Musil's affectionately ironic term for the Austro-Hungarian Empire makes clear how appealing he found the ideal of a multiethnic polity in which German language and culture may have been one, but was by no means the sole, strand. In spite of the long history of Austrian anti-Semitism, S. Y. Agnon (1888–1970), a lifelong Zionist who is widely regarded as the greatest Hebrew novelist of the twentieth century, spoke for many eastern European Jews when he described one of his characters as a native of Habsburg Austria, "where one is less conscious of the Exile and where one's thoughts are drawn to happier things."[33] The pluralism of Franz Joseph's polyglot empire was certainly far more congenial to Celan's sensibility than were any of the ethnically defined, nationalistic states that replaced it. In post-Habsburg Czernowitz, though, where the official language of government and education throughout Celan's childhood was Romanian, German was a choice, not an inheritance. In effect, Czernowitz's Jews had no "natural language," and to master High German, as Celan's mother made sure that he did, was a deliberate and entirely self-conscious accomplishment. Neither his father's emphasis on a Zionist and Hebraic education, which Celan rejected as soon as he was able, nor the Romanian of the majority of his countrymen ever penetrated as deeply as did the "motherword" of Friederike Antschel's literary German. The elective affinity binding mother and son to German meant that Celan's imagination found its truest expression in a language that was rich in cultural opportunities but also somewhat estranged from daily speech. The startling movement among different image registers and literary traditions is present even in Celan's very early poetry, well before the loss of his parents and his childhood world in the Shoah. The way in which he simultaneously draws upon Middle High German, biblical Hebrew, Romanian folk songs, and French surrealism becomes less mysterious if we think of him not so much as a German poet, but as a belated inheritor of the Habsburg linguistic and cultural heterogeneity.

Because German was the tongue chosen for him by his mother, not a given of his environment, Celan's relationship to it, even before its defilement during the Nazi years, was both more self-conscious and more charged than that of a native German for whom defining himself within the language was never open to question. After the Shoah, however, Celan's affiliation with German meant that what he most longed to preserve (the memory of his childhood world, and especially of his mother) was the very thing he most needed to shed in order to survive emotionally. Simply put, Celan could not distance himself from the injuries inflicted in and through the German language without at the same time losing himself, without abandoning everything he had become at the behest of his mother, the very person he longed to safeguard from oblivion. Injury and reparation *had* to but *could not* take place in the same tongue. In this entirely personal but also widely shared crisis, in this fusion of psychic and linguistic self-fracturing, Celan's verse incarnates the moral and esthetic dilemma facing all postwar European, and not merely Jewish, writing. If authors such as the Austrian concentration camp survivor Jean Améry (born Hans Meyer) feared that "no bridge led from death in Auschwitz to *Death in Venice*,"[34] Celan's questioning reaches deeper precisely because it is haunted not by the chasm, but rather by the continuity, and even the complicity, between the Nazi atrocities and the highest forms of Western literary and intellectual expression. For Celan, death "is a master from Germany," but he is a master whose works encompass not merely the ovens of Auschwitz. The line also suggests the great medieval German mystic, Meister Eckhart (c.1260–1327), with whose writings, especially his translations of Isaiah, Celan was intimately familiar, as well as Johann Sebastian Bach, the towering perfection of whose *Art of the Fugue* is directly invoked in the poem's title, "Death Fugue," and Goethe's *Apprenticeship of Wilhelm Meister*, the celebrated novel of the civilizing power of education and experience. Tormented by the kinship between such consummate and such lethal mastery, Celan never ceased asking both himself and his language a sharper, more urgent version of the question T. S. Eliot posed in "Gerontion": "After such knowledge, what forgiveness?"[35]

Surprisingly, in this most private and indirect of writers, details of Celan's personal history often coincide eerily with the most ominous public events. Thus it was exactly on November 9, 1938, called *Kristallnacht*, or "the night of broken glass"—when 91 Jews were killed, hundreds seriously injured, about 25,000 rounded up and later sent to concentration camps, and more than 177 synagogues and 7,500 Jewish businesses gutted or otherwise demolished by government-incited mobs—that Celan's train from Romania to France passed through one of Berlin's principal stations. The violence of *Kristallnacht* clearly anticipated the far worse savagery to come, and Celan later recalled that moment in one of the most powerfully earned, laconic images of historical foreshadowing in modern verse:

Über Krakau
bist du gekommen, am Anhalter
Bahnhof
floß deinen Blicken ein Rauch zu,
der war schon von morgen.
            "La Contrescarpe"

Via Cracow
you came, at the Anhalter
Station
you caught sight of smoke
that was already from tomorrow.
                    "La Contrescarpe"[36]

But even if, as in this case, we know the principal situations and their dates and can establish their relation to specific images in his verse, Celan's personality and temperament remain essentially elusive. Accounts of what prompted him, while he was living in Bucharest between 1945 and 1947, to adopt the name "Celan" are little more than suppositions, and we lack all but the most elementary information about his decision in 1955 to marry Gisèle de Lestrange, a graphic artist from an old French Catholic family, whose mother entered a Breton convent as soon as her husband, Gisèle's father, died. The episodes of depression and rage that led Celan in the late 1960s not merely to live apart from Gisèle and their son, Eric, but also to seek out radical treatments like electroshock therapy have not given rise to a small library of voyeuristic anecdotes. Nonetheless, from the story of his parents' arrest and deportation from Czernowitz in 1942 to his own 1970 death by drowning in the Seine, multiple and contradictory suppositions have been circulated about virtually every major event in Celan's life. It is both astonishing and salutary to acknowledge how little we can actually say with any confidence about him. Much of our ignorance is no doubt due to the way Celan's surviving friends continue to respect the poet's own reticence, and in an age when gossip has become our culture's way of talking to and about itself, there is something altogether admirable in honoring such discretion. Still, so protective a stance has a negative side to it as well, encouraging, perhaps erroneously, an excessive emphasis on what little information has become available. Paradoxically, the combination of extensive discussion of some parts of Celan's private life—in particular, the often crippling intensity of his fears about resurgent anti-Semitism and the depth to which he was shaken by Claire Goll's absurd accusations that he had plagiarized from the work of her late husband, the Alsatian Jewish poet Yvain Goll (1891–1950)—may make us overlook other, equally significant biographical clues. Since our comprehension of many of Celan's later texts often increases enormously the more we know about the circumstances of their composition, it is frustrating not to have that elucidation finally made available. How much, for example, does an image like "Magnetische Bläue im Mund, / erkeuchst du Pol um Pol" (Magnetic blue in your mouth / you gasp up pole after pole)[37] owe to the specifics of the shock treatment Celan underwent in February 1967? And were there any specific, new acts of perfidy, real or imagined, that prompted terrible outcries such as this one:

Ich schreite deinen Verrat aus,
Fußspangen an
allen Seins—
gelenken . . .

I stride out [through] your betrayal
foot-shackles on
every limb
of being

or

I pace out your betrayal
anklets on
all joints
of being[38]

Friends and biographers are naturally protective of Celan, but their guardedness has unwittingly helped to further the impression of the writer as almost preternaturally fragile. Yet here, if anywhere, the distinction between the man and the poet is decisive. Of Celan's personal vulnerability there is, alas, all too clear a record, though his survival in the Romanian slave labor brigades and his determination to risk an illegal and potentially dangerous wintertime escape from Bucharest to Vienna show a marked physical resilience and willpower that is too often overlooked in considerations of his character. As a writer, however, there was nothing at all fragile about him. Indeed, what is most evident in his mature work, both in his own texts and in his matchless translations into German of Russian, French, English, and Italian writers, is Celan's certainty of his powers. Celan knew that he was a strong enough poet to surpass both the famous nineteenth-century German translations of Shakespeare's sonnets and the enormously influential modern version by Stefan George. He knew himself sufficiently strong to compose poems as deliberate *Widerrufe* (literally, "recantations" or "disavowals"), new lyrics that are open challenges to and reworkings of cherished texts by Hölderlin and Rilke, the two German poets he most admired. The relationship I mentioned earlier between "Tenebrae" and Hölderlin's "Patmos" is merely one example among many of Celan's direct confrontation with of one of the best-known and most powerful poems in the very tradition with which he partially aligns himself. "Patmos" begins with the ringing declaration:

Nah ist
Und schwer zu fassen der Gott

Wo aber Gefahr ist, wächst
Das Rettende auch.

     Near
and hard to grasp is the God
Yet where there is danger, also grows
that which saves [rescues].[39]

In "Tenebrae," by contrast, it is "we," the murdered Jewish people who "are near,
Lord, / near and at hand," and for them it is too late to speak of "das Rettende"
which will save them. We have no formal term in American poetry like the German
Widerruf, but Wallace Stevens's reworking, in a bleaker, more astringent mode, of
Keats is precisely analogous to Celan's long dialogue-agon with Hölderlin and
Rilke. Most important, Celan was certain enough of his gifts that, when the need
arose, he could discard all the techniques of densely compacted word formation,
the neologisms and the dizzying paradoxes he had made uniquely his own. Toward
the end of his life, as a result of his one trip to Israel in 1969, Celan composed some
of the most astonishingly direct, sexually charged poems in the language. For a poet
who took such brilliant advantage of German's capacity for lexical and syntactic
metamorphoses, the way several discrete nouns can be combined to constitute a
never-before-seen compound, there is something breathtaking in the explicitness
of a late lyric such as "There stood":

Es stand
der Feigensplitter auf deiner Lippe,

es stand
Jerusalem um uns,

es stand
der Hellkiefernduft
überm Dänenschiff, dem wir dankten,

ich stand
in dir.
                         "Es stand"

There stood
a splinter of fig on your lip,

there stood
Jerusalem around us,

there stood
the bright pine scent
above the Danish skiff we thanked

I stood
in you.

                          "There stood"⁴⁰

In the original, the last two lines can also mean "I was erect / in you" with all the
immediate, sexual force of the image. But the most audacious moment of his whole
Jerusalem cycle comes when he unites the voice of a lover, a worshiper, and a child
gently laid to rest into a single benediction, in "The Poles":

sag, daß Jerusalem *ist,*

sags, als wäre ich dieses
dein Weiß,
als wärst du
meins,

als könnten wir ohne uns wir sein,

ich blättre dich auf, für immer,

du betest, du bettest
uns frei.

                          "Die Pole"

say, that Jerusalem *is,*

say it, as if I were this
your whiteness,
as if you were
mine,

as if without us we could be we,

I leaf you open, for ever,

you pray, you lay
us free.

                          "The Poles"⁴¹

When, in an explicit allusion to the Song of Songs, and perhaps also to Whitman's
Leaves of Grass, the image of the beloved's body, reverently opened like a holy book,

modulates into a pun of such explosive force—a single consonant ("t") bridging the sacred and the sexual (*du betest, du bettest;* "you pray, you lay")—we are hearing a poet utterly confident in his artistry.[42] Indeed, throughout his oeuvre, Celan is often shockingly vivid in his use of sexual imagery, sometimes in the most unlikely contexts, just as he is also often manically comic in verbal transmutations that clearly owe as much to his early involvement with surrealism as to his later Kabbalistic readings about the numinous energy latent in every letter of the alphabet. But just as there is no need always to refer each detail of Celan's writing back to his anguish as the exemplary Jewish survivor-poet, it is even more limiting to read him as though all of his work were a versified confrontation with Heidegger and a prefiguration of deconstruction. Poem after poem, from the first volume to major late achievements like the "The Poles," make clear the needlessly reductive premise of declarations like Lacoue-Labarthe's that "the entirety of Celan's poetry is a dialogue with Heidegger."[43] As a way of reading *any* strong poet, no matter how theoretically self-conscious about his language and craft, and irrespective of how deeply engaged he may be with fundamental philosophical questions, such a claim seems far-fetched; in the case of Celan, I think it bears only a slightly closer relationship to his oeuvre than does Heidegger's essay on Van Gogh's *Old Shoes with Laces* to the actual painting. (If one were inclined to trace such critical genealogies, I think a case could be made that Scholem was nearly as important an instigation for Celan's later poetry as was Heidegger, even if—or, more accurately, precisely because—Scholem's presence is more mediated and subterranean.) I am certainly not slighting the effect of Celan's reading of Heidegger, a reading that started as early as 1951 and involved a careful attention to several of Heidegger's principal books. It is clear that no contemporary thinker resonated for Celan with as charged a combination of deep sympathy and revulsion as did Heidegger. But judging by the underlinings in Celan's own copies of Heidegger, it appears that what attracted him most were Heidegger's essays on Hölderlin and Rilke, poets who were already at the center of Celan's imaginative universe.[44] Heidegger's genuine reverence for these poets, his passionate commitment to their philosophical significance, and the decisive role of poetry in Heidegger's later thinking all meant an enormous amount to Celan. So, too, and in corresponding proportion, did the ignominy of Heidegger's postwar silence about his complicity, as a onetime Nazi sympathizer, in the fate of European Jewry. Heidegger, I think, ultimately became a symbolic figure for Celan, someone who mattered as much for what he represented in Celan's internal debate about the meaning of German culture and history as for the actual tenets of his philosophy. After the two men finally met following Celan's July 24, 1967, reading at the University of Freiburg, Celan wrote a line in Heidegger's guest book at the Black Forest cottage in which he refers to the philosopher's famous garden well with its star-shaped cube at the top: "Into the hut-book, looking at the well-star, with a hope for the coming word in the heart."[45] Celan's sentence shows the profound longing he felt for some expression of contrition on Heidegger's part for having failed to say or do anything to distance himself from the Nazis when such words and deeds might have made a difference. At the very least, Celan hoped that Heidegger would offer an explanation of why not even the postwar accounts of the full magnitude of the Shoah compelled him to confront openly either his own or his country's recent past. "Todtnauberg," the much-analyzed poem Celan subsequently wrote about his encounter with Heidegger, adapts the entry from the guest book as the fulcrum of the whole piece:

> die in das Buch
> —wessen Namen nahms auf
> vor dem meinen? —,
> die in dies Buch
> geschriebene Zeile von
> einer Hoffnung, heute,
> auf eines Denkenden
> kommendes
> Wort
> im Herzen
>   "Todtnauberg"

> the line
> —whose name did the book
> register before mine? —,
> the line inscribed
> in that book about
> a hope, today,
> a thinker's
> coming
> word
> in the heart
>   "Todtnauberg"[46]

The "thinker" never uttered the "word in the heart" for which Celan longed, and when Celan published this poem in *Force of Light* he removed a crucial line from an earlier version in which, overhopeful for once, he had described Heidegger's explanatory "word" not merely as "coming" but as "un- / delayed."[47]

Celan, though, is more than just the preeminent poet of the Shoah or the author of the most searching postwar German lyrics on language and Being, even if many of the finest responses to his poetry both here and in Europe continue to be cast exclusively in terms of these two concerns. Celan was clearly also the young Éluard-inspired surrealist of the immediate postwar months in Bucharest and

Vienna, and the triumphantly erotic poet of the late Jerusalem poems. Criticism operates with antinomies that the imagination has little interest in obeying. All of Celan's writing testifies to an intense and intensely literary ambition.[48] He is as ready to use New Testament themes and motifs as to adapt passages from the Hebrew Bible, and medieval German poetry is as decisive for his writing as are Kabbalah, the foundational texts of Western mysticism, or Heideggerian philosophy. Most unsettling of all, for readers who want their great writers to exemplify an elevating single-mindedness, Celan was a writer whose powers of verbal invention come through in moments of pure textual self-affirmation, in images, word coinings, and rhythmic figures that seem to rejoice simply in being there on the page with a kind of sovereign independence of the poem's subject matter. It is the same quality that enabled Milton to be grief-wracked by the death of Edward King, and yet, in "Lycidas," to compose the most allusive and formally intricate elegy in the English language to express his grief.

As a poet, Celan was syncretistic in his interests and sources, and he approached his different projects with a fastidiousness born of strength, not fragility. Some of his power to both shock and move us is due to the ruthlessness with which he refused to accommodate expectations. Paramount among those expectations is our longing for the artist as bearer of a transcendent word through which the savagery, the shabbiness and the banality of the age will somehow find redemption. This is a debilitatingly sentimental typology to wish upon any modern poet, and it points to a host of ill-conceived assumptions in the rhetoric of unrelenting philosophical gravitas that has become a staple of recent Celan criticism. It is probably unwise to insist upon the sacerdotal function of even the greatest writers, and there is little evidence that doing so with Celan has done much to deepen the quality of responses to his poems. Because interpreting a gnomic seer is also a distinctly more glamorous activity than commenting upon a maker of poems, no doubt this self-flattering aspect is not without its own influence on critical strategies. Put as starkly as possible, what we need, I think, is a secular and *literary* reading of Celan, one that engages the enormous difficulty of his works without the pathos or evasion of a critical rhetoric permanently pitched in extremis.

Ganz und gar nicht hermetisch, "absolutely not hermetic":[49] this is what Celan insisted about his poetry, and he reacted with anger to any commentary that emphasized how inaccessible much of his writing had become, especially the poems beginning with *Atemwende (Breathturn)*, which appeared in 1967. But Celan's later style *is* hermetic, almost in the technical sense of summoning arcane knowledge and powers through word magic. (Again, it is fascinating to observe that it is often the same critics who tease out the etymological, philosophical, or Kabbalistic references in some of Celan's neologisms who then straightforwardly echo the poet's claim that a sufficiently attentive series of rereadings would yield up the poem's meaning without the need for these same external guideposts.) There are clearly poems whose meaning is fully recoverable only through intimate familiarity with Celan's private reading matter and the most circumstantial details of his daily routine. Poems often spring from specific, quotidian occurrences like crumbs of conversation, railway journeys, moments in a museum, entries in guest books, or an exchange of letters. Celan's conviction that the reader can make all the necessary links by repeated readings, without needing the personal facts or associations that initially triggered the poem, is often, but not always, justified. Moments of incomprehension are not always signs of a resistance to Celan's originality, nor need they bespeak a refusal to admit the gravity of his themes. It is worth recalling that no less scrupulous a reader than Primo Levi confessed himself deeply frustrated by Celan's "obscurity." As is true of poems like Pound's *Cantos*, many of these kinds of obscurities in Celan will undoubtedly be clarified as more information becomes available. I am not convinced, though, that even a detailed, line-by-line commentary of the type associated with editions of the classical Greek and Latin poets will ever—or even *should*—resolve a sense of foreignness, of a steadily growing inner distance at the core of Celan's later speech.

"Language doesn't only build bridges into the world, but also into loneliness."[50] This is how Celan, in 1952, described what his time trying to survive as a poet and a human being in the labor camps had taught him. In a very real sense, one of the things that his writing set about doing, from the mid 1960s, was to give that loneliness an ever more precise language and dwelling place. By comparison to his mature writing, an early masterpiece such as "Death Fugue" is still too much the "virtuoso poem," too unself-questioning in its rhetoric and its metrics for the astringency Celan increasingly began to demand as evidence of adequate poetic and personal probity. Celan began to think of his poems as inhabiting a place "north of the future,"[51] where it was still possible to sing songs "beyond humankind."[52] But to write such songs meant to transform not only the kinds of words, but also the kind of silence that filled his earlier poetry. The later poems seem to engage more than language, and they leave one with the sense that language did not continue to work, or at least no longer worked well enough. Celan often said that his poems require not just a reader, but an intimate, "an addressable you"[53] who is as indispensable to the existence of the poem as the poet himself. The one thing you cannot do in utter solitude is have a meaningful silence. (Think, for a moment, how charged with significance silence can be between lovers, and how empty of content the silence becomes when one has lost one's love and survives alone. Silence is also a doing, not just a saying, and it requires a partner.) Without the hope of dialogue, without, that is, the felt presence of other voices on *this* side of humankind, the nature of silence itself is dreadfully changed.

Before, it was not just the emotional proximity of the dead that infused Celan's poems with silence, as though giving them a space in which to still exist. The silence was also eloquent with the hope of bringing those extinguished voices into contact with new, living ones. In his later poems, when even the dream of a genuinely responsive readership fades, it is as though silence were becoming gradually speechless, as though it were no longer one of Celan's distinctive ways of saying, but a sign of the impossibility of saying anything that still matters in human accents. And yet, for all their opacity, these final texts contain some of Celan's most darkly radiant moments. "Count up what was bitter and kept you awake"[54] is what Celan instructed himself to do in an early poem. The results of that painful "counting up" will now keep readers awake for generations to come.

Notes

Exigencies of space made it impossible to acknowledge all the critics from whose writings I have benefited throughout my work on these authors. But the fact that I have been able to mention only those works from which I have directly quoted does not in any way minimize my sense of indebtedness to the wealth of thoughtful commentaries and analyses from which I have learned and without which I could never have presumed to write such a work.

To make this book as useful as possible, both to experienced scholars and to readers who do not know German, I have cited, wherever possible, both the standard German editions and the most readily available English translations of the passages quoted. Occasionally, I have silently amended the received translation when clarity or my immediate context required it. Any translations not attributed to a specific source are my own.

Introduction

1. Émile Zola, *L'Oeuvre* (Paris: Gallimard, 1983), p. 303; *The Masterpiece*, trans. Thomas Walton (Ann Arbor: University of Michigan Press, 1968), p. 268.

2. I have analyzed the evolution and logic of the modernist masterpiece in more detail in "Making Modernist Masterpieces," *Modernism/Modernity* 5, no. 3 (September 1998): 1–17.

3. William Butler Yeats, "The Choice," in *The Collected Poems* (New York: Macmillan, 1974), p. 242.

4. Honoré de Balzac, *La Comédie Humaine*, 10 vols. (Paris: Bibliothèque de la Pléiade, 1951). The citation is from vol. 1, p. ix.

5. Cf. Hegel's dictum that Napoleon was "Der Weltgeist am Pferd" (the world-spirit on horseback).

6. The phrase *faire concurrence à l'Etat-Civil* is from the "Avant-Propos" to *La Comédie Humaine*, vol. 1, p. 6.

7. Stéphane Mallarmé, "Crise De Vers," in *Oeuvres Complètes* (Paris: Bibliothèque de la Pléiade, 1945), pp. 363–64.

8. Stéphane Mallarmé, "Le Livre, Instrument Spirituel," in *Oeuvres Complètes*, p. 378. The italics in the translation are mine. It is worth noting here that I am not denying a strong element of irony on Mallarmé's part; indeed, Mallarmé's whole

formulation at the beginning of this piece suggests an ironic distance from his own apothegm, but I believe that by an entirely characteristic Mallarméan turn, the irony only intensifies, rather than undermines, his theoretical absolutism.

9. Walter Benjamin, "The Task of the Translator," in *Selected Writings: Volume 1. 1913–1926*, ed. Marcus Bullock and Michael Jennings (Cambridge, Mass.: Harvard University Press, 1996), p. 259.

10. Quoted in Richard Ellmann, *James Joyce* (New York: Oxford University Press, 1983), pp. 435–36.

11. The concept of the "death of the author" is, in any case, largely a critical refraction of Mallarmé's insistence in "Crise De Vers" that "the pure work implies the rhetorical disappearance of the poet who abandons the initiative to words" (*Oeuvres Complètes*, p. 366).

12. Charles Baudelaire, in *Curiosités esthétiques, L'Art romantique, et autres Oeuvres critiques*, ed. Henri Lemaitre (Paris: Garnier Frères, 1962), pp. 467–68. See Walter Benjamin's discussion of this very motif in his *Charles Baudelaire: A Lyric Poet in the Era of High Capitalism*, trans. Harry Zohn (London: Verso Books, 1983), pp. 81–83.

13. James Joyce, *Finnegans Wake* (New York: Viking Press, 1958), p. 186.

14. Joyce said this to Jacques Benoîst-Méchin, the French translator of "Penelope." Quoted in Ellmann, *James Joyce*, p. 521.

15. Walter Cahn, *Masterpieces: Chapters on the History of an Idea* (Princeton, N.J.: Princeton University Press, 1979), p. 122. Cahn uses the term to describe the rhetorical strategy of eighteenth-century critics, rather than artists themselves, but it seems to me to apply with still more justice to the creators of the modernist masterpieces.

16. James C. Scott, *Seeing Like a State: How Certain Schemes to Improve the Human Condition Have Failed* (New Haven, Conn.: Yale University Press, 1998). For a fascinating study of the Bolshevik state as a modernist project to make a single "artistic" whole out of every detail of public life, see Boris Groys, *The Total Art of Stalinism: Avant-Garde, Aesthetic Dictatorship, and Beyond*, trans. Charles Rougle (Princeton, N.J.: Princeton University Press, 1992).

17. Ellmann, *James Joyce*, p. 703.

18. Leo Bersani, *The Culture of Redemption* (Cambridge, Mass.: Harvard University Press, 1990).

19. James Joyce, *Ulysses* (New York: Random House, 1986), p. 156. Martin Heidegger, "Aus der Erfahrung des Denkens," in *Gesamtausgabe: Ausgabe letzter Hand*, vol. 13, ed. Hermann Heidegger (Frankfurt: Klostermann, 1976), p. 81; "The Thinker as Poet," in *Poetry, Language, Thought*, trans. Albert Hofstadter (New York: Harper and Row, 1971), p. 9.

20. Robert Musil, *Tagebücher*, 2 vols., ed. Adolf Frisé (Reinbek: Rowohlt, 1976), vol. 1, p. 896; *Diaries: 1899–1942*, selected and trans. Philip Payne (New York: Basic Books, 1998), p. 432.

21. Robert Musil, "Über den Essay," in *Prosa und Stücke, Kleine Prosa, Aphorismen, Autobiographisches, Essays und Reden, Kritik,* ed Adolf Frisé (Reinbek: Rowohlt, 1978), p. 1335; "On the Essay," in *Precision and Soul,* trans. and ed. Burton Pike and David S. Luft (Chicago: University of Chicago Press, 1990), p. 49.

22. Robert Musil,"Die Schwärmer," in *Prosa und Stücke,* p. 314; *The Enthusiasts,* trans. Andrea Simon (New York: Performing Arts Journal Publications, 1983), p. 19.

Chapter 1

1. Rainer Maria Rilke, "Erstes Buch: Das Buch vom mönchischen Leben," in *Sämtliche Werke,* 6 vols., ed. Ruth Sieber-Rilke and Ernst Zinn (Frankfurt: Insel Verlag, 1955), vol. 1, p. 301.

2. Rainer Maria Rilke, letter of September 5, 1902, in *Briefe,* 2 vols., ed. Horst Nalewski (Frankfurt: Insel Verlag, 1991), vol. 1, pp. 136–37; *Selected Letters 1902–1926,* trans. R. F. C. Hull (London: Quartet Books, 1988), pp. 10–11.

3. Rainer Maria Rilke, "Die Rosenschale," in *Sämtliche Werke,* vol. 1, p. 554; "The Bowl of Roses," in *New Poems [1907],* trans. Edward Snow (New York: North Point Press, 1984), pp. 196–97.

4. Rainer Maria Rilke, letter of August 8, 1903, in *Briefe,* vol. 1, p. 153; *Selected Letters,* p. 34 (cf. "Schon als ich zu Rodin ging, suchte ich das" [I was already looking for that when I went to Rodin]).

5. Rainer Maria Rilke, "Die Neunte Elegie," in *Sämtliche Werke,* vol. 1, p. 718; "The Ninth Elegy," in *The Selected Poetry of Rainer Maria Rilke,* trans. Stephen Mitchell (New York: Random House, 1982), pp. 199, 201.

6. Rainer Maria Rilke, "Die Siebente Elegie," in *Sämtliche Werke,* vol. 1, p. 711. Mitchell chooses, unfortunately in my judgment, to translate the line as "Nowhere, Beloved, will world be but within us" (*Selected Poetry,* p. 189).

7. T. S. Eliot, "Little Gidding," in *The Complete Poems and Plays, 1909–1950* (New York: Harcourt, Brace, 1971), p. 145. J. P. Stern, in *The Dear Purchase: A Theme in German Modernism* (Cambridge: Cambridge University Press, 1995), sees a greater affinity than do I between the *Duino Elegies* and Eliot's *Four Quartets,* but his specific observations are always suggestive.

8. Robert Musil, "Rede zur Rilke-Feier in Berlin," in *Prosa und Stücke,* pp. 1236, 1229; "Address at the Memorial Service for Rilke in Berlin," in *Precision and Soul,* pp. 244, 239.

9. Ralph Freedman, *Life of a Poet: Rainer Maria Rilke* (New York: Farrar, Straus and Giroux, 1996), p. 266.

10. Rainer Maria Rilke, "Herbsttag," in *Sämtliche Werke,* vol. 1, p. 398; "Autumn Day," in *The Book of Images,* trans. Edward Snow (New York: North Point Press, 1991), p. 79.

11. Rainer Maria Rilke, "Archäischer Torso Apollos," in *Sämtliche Werke*, vol. 1, p. 557; "Archaic Torso of Apollo," in *New Poems [1908]: The Other Part*, trans. Edward Snow (New York: North Point Press, 1987), p. 3.

12. Wycliffe is translating the Latin *per viscera misericordiae Dei nostri*, which the King James version renders as "Through the tender mercy of our God."

13. Rainer Maria Rilke, "Die neunte Elegie," in *Sämtliche Werke*, vol. 1, p. 720; "The Ninth Elegy," in Mitchell's *Selected Poetry*, pp. 201, 203.

14. Rainer Maria Rilke, letter of October 27, 1915, in *Briefe*, ed. Ruth Sieber-Rilke and Karl Altheim (Wiesbaden: Insel Verlag, 1950), p. 510; *Selected Letters*, p. 263. Unfortunately, Rilke's letters have not been systematically edited and published in a uniform edition, and so at times I have had to refer to the older one-volume edition by Sieber-Rilke and Altheim rather than to the more recent two-volume edition by Nalewski.

15. Hannah Arendt, *Rahel Varnhagen, Lebensgeschichte einer deutschen Jüdin aus der Romantik* (Munich: Piper, 1959), pp. 21–22; *Rahel Varnhagen: The Life of a Jewish Woman*, trans. Richard and Clara Winston (New York: Harcourt, Brace, Jovanovich, 1974), pp. 10–11.

16. Magda von Hattingberg, *Rilke and Benvenuta: An Intimate Correspondence*, trans. Joel Agee (New York: Fromm International, 1987), p. 59.

17. Rainer Maria Rilke, "Requiem: Für eine Freundin," in *Sämtliche Werke*, vol. 1, p. 654; "Requiem for a Friend," in Mitchell's *Selected Poetry*, p. 85.

18. Robert Hass, introduction to Mitchell's *Selected Poetry*, p. xxxii.

19. Quoted by Hass, ibid.

20. Rainer Maria Rilke, letter of May 14, 1904, in *Briefe*, ed. Nalewski, vol. 1, p. 193; *Selected Letters*, p. 425.

21. Rainer Maria Rilke, "Die Aufzeichnungen des Malte Laurids Brigge," in *Sämtliche Werke*, vol. 6, p. 930; *The Notebooks of Malte Laurids Brigge*, trans. M. D. Herter Norton (New York: Capricon Books, 1958), p. 203.

22. Rainer Maria Rilke, "Die vierte Elegie," in *Sämtliche Werke*, vol. 1, p. 697; "The Fourth Elegy," in Mitchell's *Selected Poetry*, p. 169.

23. Rainer Maria Rilke, "Die Sonette an Orpheus" (Zweiter Teil, XIII), in *Sämtliche Werke*, vol. 1, p. 759; "The Sonnets to Orpheus" (II, 13), in Mitchell's *Selected Poetry*, p. 245.

24. Rainer Maria Rilke, letter of December 28, 1911, in *Briefe*, ed. Nalewski, vol. 1, p. 370; *Selected Letters*, p. 186.

25. Rainer Maria Rilke, letters of December 19, 1912, and October 21, 1913, in *Briefe*, ed. Sieber-Rilke and Altheim, pp. 387, 411; *Selected Letters*, pp. 227, 235.

26. For a subtly nuanced psychoanalytic interpretation of this issue, see Jeanne Wolff Bernstein, "Aloneness, Loneliness, and Solitude: States of Being with Oneself as seen through the works of Vermeer, Degas, and Hopper," forthcoming.

27. Auden, W. H. "Who's Who," in *Collected Shorter Poems, 1927–1957* (New York: Random House, 1966), p. 78.

28. Marie von Thurn und Taxis, *Erinnerungen an Rainer Maria Rilke* (Frankfurt: Insel Verlag, 1966), pp. 48–49. See Mitchell's "Notes" to *Selected Poetry*, p. 315. Mitchell's translation deliberately modifies the hieratic grandiloquence of the description which I have tried to restore in the version printed here.

29. Freedman, *Life of a Poet*, p. 54.

30. Edward Snow, introduction to *Uncollected Poems* (New York: North Point Press, 1996), p. xi.

31. Ibid.

32. Rainer Maria Rilke, "An Lou Andreas-Salomé, III," in *Sämtliche Werke*, vol. 2, pp. 39–40; "To Lou Andreas Salomé, III," in Snow's *Uncollected Poems*, pp. 13, 15.

33. Rainer Maria Rilke, "Vorfrühling," in *Sämtliche Werke*, vol. 2, p. 158; "Early Spring," in Snow's *Uncollected Poems*, p. 179.

34. Lou Andreas-Salomé, *The Freud Journal*, trans. Stanley A. Leavy (London: Quartet Books, 1987), p.180.

35. Rainer Maria Rilke, "Die Sonette an Orpheus" (Zweter Teil, XIII), in *Sämtliche Werke*, vol. 1, p. 759.

36. Ibid.; "Sonnets to Orpheus" (II, 13), in Mitchell's *Selected Poetry*, pp. 244–45.

37. Rainer Maria Rilke, "Die vierte Elegie," in *Sämtliche Werke*, vol. 1, p. 697; "The Fourth Elegy," in Mitchell's *Selected Poetry*, p. 169.

38. Rainer Maria Rilke, "Die zweite Elegie," in *Sämtliche Werke*, vol. 1, p. 690; "The Second Elegy," in Mitchell's *Selected Poetry*, p. 157.

39. Rainer Maria Rilke, "An die Musik," in *Sämtliche Werke*, vol. 2, p. 111; "To Music," in Snow's *Uncollected Poems*, p. 129.

40. Simone Weil, *Gravity and Grace*, trans. Emma Craufurd (London: Routledge and Kegan Paul, 1952), p. 116.

41. Rainer Maria Rilke, "Überfließende Himmel verschwendeter Sterne," in *Sämtliche Werke*, vol. 2, p. 54; "Overflowing heavens of squandered stars," in Snow's *Uncollected Poems*, p. 57.

42. Rainer Maria Rilke, "Ach, nicht getrennt sein," in *Sämtliche Werke*, vol. 2, p. 184; "Ah, not to be cut off," in Snow's *Uncollected Poems*, p. 219.

Chapter 2

1. Robert Musil, *Der Mann ohne Eigenschaften. Roman*, 2 vols., ed. Adolf Frisé (Reinbek: Rowohlt, 1978); *The Man without Qualities*, 2 vols., trans. Sophie Wilkins and Burton Pike (New York: Alfred A. Knopf, 1995). All subsequent references are to these editions and will be acknowledged with the German volume and page number first (as *MoE*), followed by the English volume and page number (as *MwQ*).

2. Stern, *Dear Purchase*, p. 182.

3. Musil, *Tagebücher*, vol. 1, p. 667; *Diaries: 1899–1942*, p. 328.

4. Musil, "Die Schwärmer," in *Prosa und Stücke*, p. 392; *The Enthusiasts*, p. 88.

5. Musil, *MoE*, vol. 1, p. 40; *MwQ*, vol. 1, p. 37.

6. Musil, *MoE*, vol. 1, p. 103; *MwQ*, vol. 1, p. 106.

7. Musil, *MoE*, vol. 1, p. 905; *MwQ*, vol. 2, p. 982. Musil here wittily inverts one of the most famous tag lines in German literature: Faust's outcry that "two souls, alas! are living in my breast / Each one longs to be severed from the other" (*Faust*, part 1, lines 1112–13).

8. Musil, *MoE*, vol. 2, p. 1094; *MwQ*, vol. 2, p. 1190.

9. Musil, "Das hilflose Europa," in *Prosa und Stücke*, p. 1092; "Helpless Europe," in *Precision and Soul*, p. 131.

10. Musil, "Der deutsche Mensch als Symptom," in *Prosa und Stücke*, p. 1359; "The German as Symptom," in *Precision and Soul*, p. 155.

11. The function of the various nicknames applied to the characters, especially to the women in the book (Diotima, Bonadea, etc.) deserves fuller consideration than it has so far received in the critical literature.

12. Musil, *MoE*, vol. 2, pp. 1130, 1084, 1089; vol. 1, p. 755; *MwQ*, vol. 2, pp. 1229, 1179, 1184, 820.

13. Musil, *MoE*, vol. 1, p. 111; *MwQ*, vol. 1, p. 115.

14. Musil, *MoE*, vol. 1, pp. 247–57; *MwQ*, vol. 1, p. 267–77.

15. Musil, *MoE*, vol. 1, p. 653; *MwQ*, vol. 1, p. 712.

16. Musil, *MoE*, vol. 1, p. 394; *MwQ*, vol. 1, p. 427.

17. W. B. Yeats, "Among School Children," in *The Collected Poems of W. B. Yeats* (New York: Macmillan, 1956), p. 214.

18. Musil, *MoE*, vol. 1, p. 394; *MwQ*, vol. 1, p. 427.

19. Musil, *MoE*, vol. 2, p. 1084; *MwQ*, vol. 2, p. 1179.

20. Musil, *Tagebücher*, vol. 1, p. 973; *Diaries: 1899–1942*, p. 485.

21. Musil, *MoE*, vol. 1, p. 89; *MwQ*, vol. 1, p. 90.

22. Musil, *MoE*, vol. 1, p. 178; *MwQ*, vol. 1, p. 190.

23. Musil, *MoE*, vol. 1, p. 741; *MwQ*, vol. 2, p. 805.

24. Musil, *MoE*, vol. 1, p. 593; *MwQ*, vol. 1, p. 647.

25. Musil, *Tagebücher*, vol. 1, p. 354; *Diaries: 1899–1942*, p. 209.

26. I have analyzed this aspect of the novel at length in *Foregone Conclusions: Against Apocalyptic History* (Berkeley: University of California Press, 1994).

27. Musil, *MoE*, vol. 1, p. 466; *MwQ*, vol. 1, p. 507.

28. Musil, *MoE*, vol. 1, pp. 20, 359; *MwQ*, vol. 1, pp. 15, 390.

29. Musil, *MoE*, vol. 1, p. 19; *MwQ*, vol. 1, p. 14.

30. Musil, *Prosa und Stücke*, p. 311; *The Enthusiasts*, p. 16.

31. Musil, *MoE*, vol. 2, p. 1084; *MwQ*, vol. 2, p. 1179.

32. Musil, *MoE*, vol. 2, p. 1090; *MwQ*, vol. 2, p. 1186.

33. Musil, *MoE*, vol. 2, p. 1084; *MwQ*, vol. 2, p. 1179.

34. Musil, *MoE*, vol. 2, p. 1089–90; *MwQ*, vol. 2, p. 1185.

35. Musil, *Tagebücher*, vol. 1, p. 973; *Diaries: 1899–1942*, p. 485.

36. Musil, *Tagebücher*, vol. 1, p.722; *Diaries: 1899–1942*, p. 378.

Chapter 3

1. Denis Diderot, *Le Neveu de Rameau*, ed. Jean Fabre (Geneva: Librarie Droz, 1963), pp. 9–12.

2. Marcel Proust, *Le Côté de Guermantes*, vol. 2 of *A la recherche du temps perdu*, 3 vols. (Paris: Bibliothèque de la Pléiade, 1954), p. 152; *The Guermantes Way*, vol. 2 of *Remembrance of Things Past*, trans. C. K. Scott Moncrieff and Terence Kilmartin, 3 vols. (New York: Random House, 1981), p. 154.

3. Martin Heidegger, *Die Selbstbehauptung der deutschen Universität* (Breslau: Wilhelm Korn Verlag, 1933); "The Self-Assertion of the German University," in *The Heidegger Controversy: A Critical Reader*, ed. Richard Wolin (Cambridge, Mass.: MIT Press, 1993), pp. 29–39.

4. Martin Heidegger, "Deutsche Studenten," in Guido Schneeberger, *Nachlese zu Heidegger* (Bern: A. G. Suhr, 1962), pp. 135–36; "German Students," in *The Heidegger Controversy*, p. 47.

5. Quoted in Rüdiger Safranski, *Martin Heidegger: Between Good and Evil*, trans. Ewald Osers (Cambridge, Mass.: Harvard University Press, 1998), p. 249.

6. Martin Heidegger, *Einführung in die Metaphysik* (Tübingen: Max Niemeyer Verlag, 1953), p. 152; *An Introduction to Metaphysics*, trans. Ralph Manheim (New Haven, Conn.: Yale University Press, 1959), p. 199.

7. Martin Heidegger, "Die Technik und die Kehre," in *Vorträge und Aufsätze* (Pfullingen: Günter Neske Verlag, 1954), pp. 13–44; "The Question Concerning Technology," in *Martin Heidegger: Basic Writings*, ed. David Farrell Krell (San Francisco: HarperSanFrancisco, 1993), pp. 311–41.

8. Martin Heidegger, "Das Ge-Stell," in *Gesamtausgabe*, vol. 79, p. 27.

9. Jürgen Habermas, *The New Conservatism*, trans. S. W. Nicolsen (Cambridge, Mass.: MIT Press, 1992), p. 159.

10. Heidegger, *Einführung in die Metaphysik*, pp. 28–29; *Introduction to Metaphysics*, p. 37.

11. Richard Rorty, "Taking Philosophy Seriously," *New Republic* 11 (April 1988): 33.

12. Berel Lang, *Heidegger's Silence* (Ithaca, N.Y.: Cornell University Press, 1996), p. 114, n. 4.

13. Martin Heidegger, "Nur noch ein Gott kann uns retten," *Der Spiegel*, 31 May 1976, p. 214; "Only a God Can Save Us," in *The Heidegger Controversy*, p. 110.

14. Heidegger, "Nur noch ein Gott," p. 212; "Only a God," pp. 20–21, 109.

15. Quoted in the introduction to *The Heidegger Controversy*, pp. vii–viii.

16. Martin Heidegger, "Was ist Metaphsik?" in *Wegmarken* (Frankfurt: Vittorio Klostermann, 1967), p. 18; "What Is Metaphysics?" in *Heidegger: Basic Writings*, p. 109.

17. Alexander Nehamas, *The Art of Living: Socratic Reflections from Plato to Foucault* (Berkeley: University of California Press, 1998), p. 1.

18. I say "supposed" because it has been extraordinarily difficult to track down the evidence for Ryle's statement. It appears in Berel Lang's *Heidegger's Silence*, p. 86. Lang (p. 125) cites Robert Bernasconi, "Habermas and Arendt on the Philosopher's 'Error,'" *Graduate Faculty Philosophy Journal* 14/15 (1991): 4. Bernasconi, though, cites a similarly but not identically phrased dismissal by Ryle, but he prefaces the quote with "Ryle . . . allegedly said early in 1960 . . ." (p. 4). Bernasconi cites as his source (p. 21) the *Times Higher Education Supplement*, no. 850, 17 February 1989, p. 12. The original source for all these versions of Ryle's supposed statement is in the "Letters to the Editor" section of the *THES* and derives from a letter by James Thrower of the University of Aberdeen. Thrower writes that early in 1960 Ryle told him, "Heidegger. Can't be a good philosopher. Wasn't a good man." It is disturbing, as well as instructive, to see how so indirect and problematic a source can be taken up and cited as though it were a definite part of a writer's legacy.

19. Hans-Georg Gadamer, quoted in Lang, *Heidegger's Silence*, p. 86.

20. Heidegger, "Nur noch ein Gott," p. 217; "Only a God," p. 113.

21. Jean-François Lyotard, *Heidegger et "les juifs"* (Paris: Galilée, 1988), p. 16.

22. Theodor Adorno, letter to *Diskus* [University of Frankfurt student newspaper], January 1963.

23. Rorty, "Taking Philosophy Seriously," p. 33.

24. Erich Jaensch, quoted in Hugo Ott, *Martin Heidegger: A Political Life*, trans. Allan Blunden (New York: Basic Books, 1993), p. 257.

25. Quoted in Lang, *Heidegger's Silence*, p. 6.

26. Heidegger, "Nur noch ein Gott," p. 209; "Only a God," p. 106.

27. Martin Heidegger, *Gelassenheit* (Pfullingen: G. Neske, 1960), p. 16; *Discourse on Thinking*, trans. John M. Anderson and E. Hans Freund (New York: Harper and Row, 1966), p. 47.

28. In the introduction to *The Heidegger Controversy*, p. xvii.

29. Martin Heidegger, "Heraklit," in *Gesamtausgabe*, vol. 55, p. 123; *The Heidegger Controversy*, p. 14.

30. Martin Heidegger, "Die Grundbegriffe der Metaphysik: Welt, Endlichkeit, Einsamkeit," in *Gesamtausgabe*, vol. 29/30, p. 19; *The Fundamental Concepts of Metaphysics: World, Finitude, Solitude*, trans. William McNeill and Nicholas Walker (Bloomington: Indiana University Press, 1995), p. 13.

31. See Safranski, *Heidegger: Between Good and Evil*, pp. 130–31, on whom my description of Heidegger's behavior at Marburg is based, for still more details about

Heidegger's determination to be treated from the very beginning of his academic career as a "mysterious star."

32. Heidegger, "Die Grundbegriffe der Metaphysik," p. 244; *Fundamental Concepts of Metaphysics*, p. 164.

33. Quoted in Safranski, *Heidegger: Between Good and Evil*, p. 188.

34. Heidegger, "Nur noch ein Gott," p. 212; "Only a God," p. 109.

35. Hannah Arendt, "Martin Heidegger ist achtzig Jahre alt," in *Menschen in finstern Zeiten* (Pfullingen: G. Neske, 1988), p. 184; "For Martin Heidegger's Eightieth Birthday," in *Martin Heidegger and National Socialism*, trans. Lisa Harries and Joachim Neugroschel, ed. Günther Neske and Emil Kettering (New York: Paragon House, 1990), p. 217.

36. Heidegger, "Nur noch ein Gott," p. 209; "Only a God," p. 106.

37. Here, the notable exception is clearly James Joyce, whose novels are virtually unique in being simultaneously committed to the creation of an all-encompassing, monumental modern masterpiece, and yet absolutely respectful of and committed to the prosaic virtues and quotidian desires of their characters.

38. Martin Heidegger, *Sein und Zeit* (Tübingen: Max Niemeyer Verlag, 1967), part 2: 59, p. 289; *Being and Time*, trans. John Maquarrie and Edward Robinson (New York: Harper and Row, 1962), p. 335.

39. Heidegger, *Sein und Zeit*, part 1: 27, p. 127; *Being and Time*, p. 165.

40. Heidegger, "Was ist Metaphysik?" p. 12; "What Is Metaphysics?" p. 103.

41. Wallace Stevens, "The Snow Man," in *The Collected Poems* (New York: Alfred A. Knopf, 1978), p. 9.

42. Heidegger, *Sein und Zeit*, part 2: 51, p. 254; *Being and Time*, p. 254.

43. Martin Heidegger, "Hölderlins Hymnen 'Germanien' und 'Der Rhein,'" in *Gesamtausgabe*, vol. 39, p. 144.

44. I owe this clarification to discussions with Brian Glaser, a graduate student in the UC Berkeley English Department, from whose lucid defense of Heidegger against some of my harsher strictures I have learned a great deal.

45. Quoted in Safranski, *Heidegger: Between Good and Evil*, p. 188.

46. Martin Heidegger, *Die Selbstbehauptung der deutschen Universität* (Frankfurt: Klosterman, 1990), pp. 38–39; Gunther Neske and Emil Kettring, *Martin Heidegger and National Socialism: Questions and Answers*, trans. Lisa Harries (New York: Paragon House, 1990), p. 29.

47. Johann Georg Hamann, from a letter of May 20, 1756, to J. G. Lindner in Hamann, *Briefwechsel*, 7 vols., ed. Walther Ziesemer and Arthur Henkel (Frankfurt: Insel Verlag, 1955–79), vol. 1, p. 202.

48. Martin Heidegger, *Was Heisst Denken?* (Tübingen: Max Niemeyer Verlag, 1971), p. 11; *What Is Called Thinking?* trans. J. Glenn Gray (New York: Harper and Row, 1968), p. 30.

49. Amos Funkenstein, "Theological Responses to the Holocaust," in *Perceptions of Jewish History* (Berkeley: University of California Press, 1993), pp. 332–33.

50. Quoted in Safranski, *Heidegger: Between Good and Evil*, p. 266. The useful term "national fundamental ontology" is Safranski's. The discussion of *Je-meinigkeit* and *Je-unsrigkeit* was first raised in Heidegger's "Logic" lectures of 1934.

51. Martin Heidegger, "Brief über den Humanismus," in *Wegmarken*, p. 325; "Letter on Humanism," in *Heidegger: Basic Writings*, p. 230.

52. I have adapted these sentences with only slight modification from Safranski, *Heidegger: Between Good and Evil*, p. 218.

53. Martin Heidegger, "The Thinker as Poet," in *Poetry, Language, Thought*, p. 4.

54. Martin Heidegger, "Warum bleiben wir in der Provinz?" in Schneeberger, *Nachlese zu Heidegger*, p. 218; "Why Do I Stay in the Provinces?" in *Heidegger: The Man and the Thinker*, ed. Thomas Sheehan (Chicago: Precedent Publishing, 1981), p. 29.

55. Martin Heidegger, "Der Ursprung des Kunstwerkes," in *Holzwege* (Frankfurt: Klostermann, 1950), pp. 18–19; "The Origin of the Work of Art," in *Poetry, Language, Thought*, trans. Albert Hofstadter (New York: Harper and Row, 1975), pp. 33–34.

56. Heidegger, "Der Ursprung des Kunstwerkes," p. 20; "Origin of the Work of Art," p. 35.

57. Interestingly enough, Heidegger himself never names the painting in question. Since there are a number of possible Van Gogh canvases, Schapiro also identifies which one Heidegger had in mind. Meyer Schapiro,"The Still Life as a Personal Object: A Note on Heidegger and van Gogh," in *The Reach of Mind: Essays in Memory of Kurt Goldstein*, ed. Marianne Simmel (New York: Springer, 1968), pp. 203–9. The passage quoted is on p. 206 of Schapiro's essay.

58. Thomas Bernhard, *Alte Meister* (Frankfurt: Suhrkamp Verlag, 1993), pp. 86–95; *Old Masters*, trans. Ewald Osers (Chicago: University of Chicago Press, 1992), pp. 41–46.

Chapter 4

1. Walter Benjamin, "Das Leben der Studenten," in *Gesammelte Schriften*, 7 vols., ed. Rolf Tiedemann and Hermann Schweppenhäuser (Frankfurt: Suhrkamp Verlag, 1974–89), vol. 2, no. 1, p. 75; "The Life of Students," in *Selected Writings: Volume 1, 1913–1926*, ed. Marcus Bullock and Michael W. Jennings (Cambridge, Mass.: Harvard University Press, 1996), pp. 37–38. I have considerably modified the translation in order to approximate more closely Benjamin's tone in this early essay.

2. Gershom Scholem, *Walter Benjamin: The Story of a Friendship*, trans. Harry Zohn (New York: Schocken Books, 1981), pp. 3–4.

3. Walter Benjamin, "Über den Begriff der Geschichte," in *Gesammelte Schriften,* vol. 1, no. 2, p. 701; "Theses on the Philosophy of History," in *Illuminations,* trans. Harry Zohn, ed. and introd. Hannah Arendt (London: Collins/Fontana Books, 1973), p. 263.

4. On the relationship between Scholem and Benjamin, especially as it increasingly found expression in their common fascination with Kafka, see Robert Alter's illuminating study, *Necessary Angels: Tradition and Modernity in Kafka, Benjamin, and Scholem* (Cambridge, Mass.: Harvard University Press, 1991).

5. Benjamin, "Über den Begriff der Geschichte," p. 704; "Theses on the Philosophy of History," p. 266.

6. Walter Benjamin, "Der Sürrealismus," in *Gesammelte Schriften,* vol. 2, no. 1, p. 306; "Surrealism," in *Reflections: Essays, Aphorisms, Autobiographical Writings,* trans. Edmund Jephcott, ed. Peter Demetz (New York: Harcourt Brace Jovanovich, 1978), p. 189.

7. Walter Benjamin, "Theologisch-Politisches Fragment," in *Gesammelte Schriften,* vol. 2, no. 1, p. 202; "Theologico-Political Fragment," in *Reflections,* p. 312.

8. Benjamin, "Über den Begriff der Geschichte," p. 697; "Theses on the Philosophy of History," p. 259.

9. Benjamin, "Über den Begriff der Geschichte," p. 695; "Theses on the Philosophy of History," p. 257.

10. Ibid.

11. Benjamin, "Über den Begriff der Geschichte," pp. 702, 698; "Theses on the Philosophy of History," pp. 264, 260.

12. Walter Benjamin, "Über einige Motive bei Baudelaire," in *Gesammelte Schriften,* vol. 1, no. 2, p. 637; *Charles Baudelaire: A Lyric Poet in the Era of High Capitalism,* trans. Harry Zohn (London: Verso Books: 1983), p. 139.

13. Benjamin, "Über den Begriff der Geschichte," p. 694; "Theses on the Philosophy of History," p. 256.

14. Max Horkheimer quoted in Rolf Tiedemann's "Historischer Materialismus und der politische Materialismus," in *Materialien zu Benjamins Thesen "Über den Begriff der Geschichte,"* ed. P. Bulthaup (Frankfurt: Suhrkamp, 1975), pp. 87–88; translated in Irving Wohlfarth's "On the Messianic Structure of Walter Benjamin's Reflections," in *Glyph,* Johns Hopkins Textual Studies 3 (Baltimore: Johns Hopkins University Press, 1978), p. 160.

15. Primo Levi, *The Drowned and the Saved,* trans. R. Rosenthal (New York: Vintage Books, 1989), pp. 24–25.

16. For an extended discussion of this idea, see Richard Sieburth's "Benjamin the Scrivener," *Assemblage* 6 (1988): 7–23.

17. Walter Benjamin, "Die Aufgabe des Übersetzers," in *Gesammelte Schriften,* vol. 4, no. 1, p. 10; "The Task of the Translator," in *Selected Writings: Volume 1, 1913–1926,* p. 254.

18. E. P. Thompson, *The Making of the English Working Class* (New York: Vintage Books, 1966), p. 12.

19. Some of the main texts in which the theory of prosaics is sketched out include Gary Saul Morson, *Hidden in Plain View: Narrative and Creative Potentials in "War and Peace"* (Stanford, Calif.: Stanford University Press, 1987) and *Narrative and Freedom: The Shadows of Time* (New Haven, Conn.: Yale University Press, 1994); Gary Saul Morson and Caryl Emerson, *Mikhail Bakhtin: Creation of a Prosaics* (Stanford, Calif.: Stanford University Press, 1990); Michael André Bernstein, *Bitter Carnival: Ressentiment and the Abject Hero* (Princeton, N.J.: Princeton University Press, 1992) and *Foregone Conclusions: Against Apocalyptic History* (Berkeley: University of California Press, 1994).

20. Walter Benjamin, "Goethes Wahlverwandtschaften," in *Gesammelte Schriften*, vol. 4, no. 1, pp. 123–201; "Goethe's Elective Affinities," in *Selected Writings: Volume 1, 1913–1926*, pp. 297–360.

21. Benjamin, "Über den Begriff der Geschichte," p. 694; "Theses on the Philosophy of History," p. 256.

22. Walter Benjamin, "Ursprung des deutschen Trauerspiels," in *Gesammelte Schriften*, vol. 1, no. 1, p. 10; *The Origin of German Tragic Drama*, trans. John Osborne (London: New Left Books, 1977), p. 166.

23. Benjamin, "Über den Begriff der Geschichte," p. 702; "Theses on the Philosophy of History," p. 264.

24. Walter Benjamin, "Letter to Herbert Belmore, June 23, 1913," in *The Correspondence of Walter Benjamin: 1910–1940*, trans. Manfred R. Jacobson and Evelyn M. Jacobson, ed. and annotated Gershom Scholem and Theodor W. Adorno (Chicago: University of Chicago Press, 1994), p. 35.

25. Walter Benjamin, "Gespräche mit Brecht," in *Versuche über Brecht*, ed. Günter Busch (Frankfurt: Suhrkamp Verlag, 1978), p. 157; "Conversations with Brecht," in *Reflections*, p. 207.

26. Benjamin, "Gespräche mit Brecht," p.158. "Conversations with Brecht," p. 208.

27. Walter Benjamin, "Letter to Gerhard Scholem, June 13, 1924," in *Correspondence of Benjamin*, p. 244.

28. Walter Benjamin, "Ankündigung der Zeitschrift: Angelus Novus," in *Gesammelte Schriften*, vol. 2, no. 1, p. 242; "Announcement of the Journal *Angelus Novus*," in *Selected Writings: Volume 1, 1913–1926*, p. 293.

29. Walter Benjamin, "Letter to Gerhard Scholem, November 27, 1921," in *Correspondence of Benjamin*, p. 196.

30. Benjamin, "Über den Begriff der Geschichte," p. 695; "Theses on the Philosophy of History," p. 257.

31. Gershom Scholem, *The Messianic Idea in Judaism* (New York: Schocken Books, 1971), p. 21.

32. Theodor Adorno, "Benjamin the Letter Writer," in *Correspondence of Benjamin,* p. xxi.

33. Quoted in Momme Brodersen, *Walter Benjamin: A Biography,* trans. Malcolm R. Green and Ingrida Ligers (London: Verso Books, 1996), p. 297, n. 76.

34. Benjamin, "Goethes *Wahlverwandtschaften,*" p. 201; "Goethe's *Elective Affinities,*" p. 356.

35. Walter Benjamin, "Letter to Gerhard Scholem, January 20, 1930," in *Correspondence of Benjamin,* p. 359.

36. Benjamin, "Über einige Motive bei Baudelaire," p. 607; *Baudelaire: Lyric Poet,* p. 111.

37. Stéphane Mallarmé, "cette donnée exacte qu'il faut, si l'on fait de la littérature, parler autrement que les journaux . . . ," in *Correspondance,* 11 vols., ed. H. Mondor and L. J. Austin (Paris: Gallimard, 1959–73), vol. 3, p. 67.

38. Brodersen, *Walter Benjamin: A Biography,* pp. 159–61.

39. Walter Benjamin, "Letter to Gerhard Scholem, July 26, 1932," in *Correspondence of Benjamin,* p. 396.

40. Walter Benjamin, "Zum Bilde Prousts," in *Gesammelte Schriften,* vol. 2, no. 1, p. 320; "The Image of Proust," in *Illuminations,* p. 214.

41. Walter Benjamin, "Letter to Gerhard Scholem, September 18, 1926," in *Correspondence of Benjamin,* p. 305.

42. Günter Anders, "Der Defekt," an outline from a proposed collection of literary essays written in April 1930. Reprinted in Brodersen, *Walter Benjamin: A Biography,* p. 183.

43. Theodor W. Adorno is quoting Benjamin in "Benjamin the Letter Writer," in *Correspondence of Benjamin,* p. xix.

44. Benjamin is quoting Jacques Rivière in "Zum Bilde Prousts," p. 322; "The Image of Proust," p. 215.

45. Walter Benjamin, "Letter to Gerhard Scholem, June 12, 1938," in *Correspondence of Benjamin,* p. 566.

Chapter 5

1. Paul Celan and Nelly Sachs, *Briefwechsel,* ed. Barbara Wiedemann (Frankfurt: Suhrkamp Verlag, 1993), p. 14; *Correspondence,* trans. Cris Clark (New York: Sheep Meadow Press, 1995), p. 6.

2. Celan is notoriously difficult to translate. No other modern German poet has presented his translators with greater difficulties, nor have the translations of any other German-language writer been as fiercely contested as those of Celan. The best English versions I know are those of John Felstiner in his carefully researched biography, *Paul Celan: Poet, Survivor, Jew* (New Haven, Conn.: Yale University Press,

1995), and wherever possible I have cited Felstiner's English versions in my text. No previous translator has made so careful and uncoercive a case for his particular rendering or integrated translation and commentary so thoughtfully. Even when I disagree with some of his decisions, Felstiner carefully explains what prompted his choice, so that a reader has sufficient information to imagine different possible solutions than Felstiner's. But it is often helpful to compare several translations, less to evaluate them on their own terms than to see how differently Celan's lines can be understood. Moreover, Felstiner's biography unfortunately often does not print a continuous complete text of either the English translation or the German original, and so I have also referred readers to the readily available one-volume work by Michael Hamburger, *Selected Poems of Paul Celan* (New York: Persea Books, 1988), as well as to Katherine Washburn's and Margaret Guillemin's *Paul Celan: Last Poems* (San Francisco: North Point Press, 1986) and Pierre Joris's *Breathturn* (Los Angeles: Sun and Moon Press, 1995).

3. Franz Kafka, *Letters to Friends, Family and Editors*, trans. Richard and Clara Winston (New York: Schocken Books, 1977), p. 289.

4. Paul Celan, *Gesammelte Werke*, 5 vols., ed. Beda Allemann and Stefan Reichert (Frankfurt: Suhrkamp Verlag, 1983), vol. 3, p. 186; *Collected Prose*, trans. Rosmarie Waldrop (Manchester: P.N. Review/Carcanet, 1986), p. 34.

5. Quoted in Israel Chalfen, *Paul Celan: A Biography of His Youth*, trans. Maximilian Bleyleben (New York: Persea Books, 1991), p. 184.

6. Felstiner, *Paul Celan*, p. 57.

7. Paul Celan, "Todesfuge," in *Gesammelte Werke*, vol. 1, p. 42; "Death Fugue," in Felstiner, *Paul Celan*, p. 31; "Death Fugue," in Hamburger, *Selected Poems*, p. 63.

8. Paul Celan, "Psalm," in *Gesammelte Werke*, vol. 1, p. 225; "Psalm," in Felstiner, *Paul Celan*, p. 167; "Psalm," in Hamburger, *Selected Poems*, p. 175.

9. Ibid.

10. Paul Celan, "Fadensonnen," in *Gesammelte Werke*, vol. 2, p. 117.

11. Paul Celan, "Assisi," in *Gesammelte Werke*, vol. 1, p. 108; "Assisi," in Felstiner, *Paul Celan*, p. 81; "Assisi," in Hamburger, *Selected Poems*, p. 83.

12. Felstiner, *Paul Celan*, p. 51.

13. Ibid.

14. Paul Celan, "Todesfuge," in *Gesammelte Werke*, vol. 1, p. 41; "Death Fugue," in Felstiner, *Paul Celan*, p. 31; "Death Fugue," in Hamburger, *Selected Poems*, p. 61.

15. The intensity of the controversy surrounding Binjamin Wilkomirski's *Fragments* is clearly linked to a similar sense of a fundamental moral, cultural, and imaginative taboo being violated. By now, it seems to me that the vehemence of Wilkomirski's defenders and attackers, particularly the extravagant claims they make for what is at stake in the question of whether his book is invented or based on his real experiences, is more interesting than the case itself.

16. Mark Rosenthal, *Anselm Kiefer* (Chicago and Philadelphia: Prestel-Verlag, 1987), p. 95.

17. Paul Taylor, "Painter of the Apocalypse," *New York Times Magazine*, 16 October 1988, p. 81.

18. Hilda Schiff, ed., *Holocaust Poetry* (New York: St. Martin's Press, 1995), pp. xviii, 209.

19. *The Notebooks of Samuel Taylor Coleridge*, 3 vols., ed. Kathleen Coburn (New York: Pantheon Books, 1957), vol. 1 (text), p. 90 (section 87G.81).

20. Paul Celan, "Schimmelgrün ist das Haus des Vergessens," from "Der Sand aus den Urnen," in *Gesammelte Werke*, vol. 1, p. 22; "Sand from the Urns," in Felstiner, *Paul Celan*, p. 50; "Sand from the Urns," in Hamburger, *Selected Poems*, p. 43.

21. Paul Celan, "wir licben einander wie Mohn und Gedächtnis, / wir schlafen wie Wein in den Muscheln, / wie das Meer im Blutstrahl des Mondes," from "Corona," in *Gesammelte Werke*, vol. 1, p. 37; "Corona," in Hamburger, *Selected Poems*, p. 58; "Corona," in Felstiner, *Paul Celan*, p. 55.

22. Paul Celan, "Welchen der Steine du hebst," in *Gesammelte Werke*, vol. 1, p. 129; "Whichever Stone You Lift," in Felstiner, *Paul Celan*, p. 71.

23. Paul Celan, "Tenebrae," in *Gesammelte Werke*, vol. 1, p. 163; "Tenebrae," in Hamburger, *Selected Poems*, p. 113; "Tenebrae," in Felstiner, *Paul Celan*, p. 101.

24. Quoted in Felstiner, *Paul Celan*, p. 101.

25. Gottfried von Strassburg, *Tristan and Isolde*, trans. A. T. Hatto (New York: Continuum, 1988), lines 15733–44, p. 207; italics mine.

26. Stéphane Mallarmé, "Le Mystère dans les lettres," in *Oeuvres Complètes*, p. 387.

27. Paul Celan, "Engführung," in *Gesammelte Werke*, vol. 1, pp. 199, 204; "Stretto," in Felstiner, *Paul Celan*, pp. 121–22, 124; "The Straightening," in Hamburger, *Selected Poems*, pp. 141, 149.

28. Paul Celan, "Aschenglorie," in *Gesammelte Werke*, vol. 2, p. 72; "Ashglory," in *Breathturn*, p. 179.

29. Paul Celan, "Der Meridian," in *Gesammelte Werke*, vol. 3, pp. 197–98; "The Meridian," in *Collected Prose*, pp. 48, 50.

30. Paul Celan, "Der Meridian," in *Gesammelte Werke*, vol. 3, p. 198; "The Meridian," in *Collected Prose*, p. 49.

31. Krzysztof Ziarek, *Inflected Language: Towards a Hermeneutics of Nearness: Heidegger, Levinas, Stevens, Celan* (Albany: State University of New York Press, 1994), p. 139.

32. Paul Celan, quoted in Felstiner, *Paul Celan*, p. 6.

33. S. Y. Agnon, "Betrothed," in *Two Tales*, trans. Walter Lever (New York: Schocken Books, 1966), p. 22.

34. Jean Améry, *At the Mind's Limits: Contemplations by a Survivor on Auschwitz and Its Realities*, trans. Sidney and Stella Rosenfeld (New York: Schocken Books, 1986), p. 16.

35. T. S. Eliot, "Gerontion," in *Complete Poems and Plays*, p. 22.

36. Paul Celan, "La Contrescarpe," in *Gesammelte Werke*, vol. 1, p. 283; "La Contrescarpe," in Felstiner, *Paul Celan*, p. 193.

37. Paul Celan, "Magnetische Bläue," in *Gesammelte Werke*, vol. 2, p. 293.

38. Paul Celan, "Ich schreite," in *Gesammelte Werke*, vol. 2, p. 401. I owe the second version of Celan's lines to my friend and colleague Thomas G. Rosenmeyer, who adds the following helpful explanation to his translation: "'Ausschreiten' is the pacing out of a distance; and a 'Spange' is commonly a broach or a bracelet. As for 'Gelenk,' again the common meaning is 'joint'; 'limb' is 'Glied,' and in any case it makes more sense to me to put the anklet on a joint, and 'being' having joints is to me a more interesting idea than the more startling anthropomorphizing of being into a congeries of limbs."

39. Friedrich Hölderlin, *Werke, Briefe, Dokumente* (Munich: Winkler-Verlag, 1969), p. 177.

40. Paul Celan, "Es stand," in *Gesammelte Werke*, vol. 3, p. 96; "There Stood," in Felstiner, *Paul Celan*, p. 268; "There Was," in *Paul Celan: Last Poems*, p. 179.

41. Paul Celan, "Die Pole," in *Gesammelte Werke*, vol. 3, p. 105; "The Poles," in Felstiner, *Paul Celan*, p. 275; "The Poles," in Hamburger, *Selected Poems*, p. 345.

42. In English, I think only Emily Dickinson regularly dares as much, although with different materials and to different effects. Consider, for example, the near blasphemy with which she links "pray" and "prate" in the opening lines of "We pray — to Heaven — / We prate — of Heaven —," in *The Complete Poems of Emily Dickinson*, ed. T. H. Johnson (Boston: Little, Brown, 1960), poem 489, p. 235.

43. Philippe Lacoue-Labarthe, *La poésie comme expérience* (Paris: Christian Bourgeois Editeur, 1986), p. 50.

44. Felstiner, *Paul Celan*, pp.72ff. provides a useful account of what passages Celan chose to underline or comment on (sometimes simply with an exclamation mark in the margin) in his personal copies of Heidegger.

45. Quoted in Felstiner, *Paul Celan*, p. 244.

46. Paul Celan, "Todtnauberg," in *Gesammelte Werke*, vol. 2, pp. 255–56; Hamburger, *Selected Poems*, p. 293; Felstiner, *Paul Celan*, p. 246.

47. For the history of "Todtnauburg'"s composition, see Felstiner, *Paul Celan*, pp. 244–47.

48. I have adopted this phrase by A. O. Scott from its very different context in his review essay, "Looking for Raymond Carver," *New York Review of Books* 46, no. 13 (12 August 1999): 53.

49. Paul Celan, quoted in Felstiner, *Paul Celan*, p. 253.

50. Felstiner, *Paul Celan*, p. 16.

51. Paul Celan, "In den Flüssen," in *Gesammelte Werke*, vol. 2, p. 14; "In the Rivers," in *Breathturn*, p. 61; "In the Rivers," in Felstiner, *Paul Celan*, p. 216.

52. Paul Celan, "Fadensonnen,"in *Gesammelte Werke,* vol. 2, p. 26; "Threadsuns," in *Breathturn,* p. 85; "Threadsuns," in Felstiner, *Paul Celan,* p. 218.

53. The phrase "an addressable you" (*ein ansprechbares Du*) is from the "Speech on the Occasion of Receiving the Literature Prize of the Free Hanseatic City of Bremen," in *Gesammelte Werke,* vol. 3, p. 186. Waldrop's *Collected Prose,* p. 35, translates it as "an approachable you," which misses precisely the element of speech and listening that was so crucial to Celan. Felstiner says "addressable thou" (*Paul Celan,* p. xvi), which is preferable, except for the needless archaism of "thou."

54. Paul Celan, "Zähle," in *Gesammelte Werke,* vol. 1, p. 78; "Count," in Hamburger, *Selected Poems,* p. 75; "Count," in Felstiner, *Paul Celan,* p. 63.

Index